WILD FRUIT

To our daughters, sons-in-law, and grandchildren.

© Éditions du Rouergue, France, 2013
This edition published in 2014 © Timber Press, Inc

Technical review of the Timber Press edition
by Dave Hamilton.

The Haseltine Building
133 S.W. Second Avenue, Suite 450
Portland, Oregon 97204-3527
timberpress.com

6a Lonsdale Road
London
NW6 6RD
timberpress.co.uk

Printed in China

ISBN 13: 978-1-60469-586-1

Catalogue records for this book are
available from the British Library
and the Library of Congress.

Photo and illustration credits appear on page 223.

ALAIN
&
MARIE-JEANNE
GÉNEVÉ

WILD FRUIT

TIMBER PRESS
Portland • London

WARNING

ADVICE FOR WILD BERRY AND FRUIT FORAGERS

Pick only precisely identified fruit. When in doubt, exercise the utmost caution. Carefully recheck all the characteristics of unfamiliar species; do not be satisfied with incomplete identification and do not take unnecessary risks.

Although nature seems bountiful, there are basic rules that should be followed to protect flora and fauna living in delicate equilibrium. You should not plunder a site under any circumstances, since animals may need these fruits to survive. Not only do we have a duty to share food sources with other species, it is also to our advantage as birds and various other small animals are an excellent means of natural propagation for a number of plant species, allowing the plants to spread and thus have a greater chance of persisting for future generations. Come spring and flowering time, these new plants will provide food for thousands of insects that feed on the pollen contained in the flowers.

LEVEL OF DANGER

Some plants pose a risk from accidental ingestion (fruits), allergenic contact (leaves, pollen) or even by causing wounds (thorns). However, it is important to keep things in perspective. The amount of poison in these situations is often minimal, and, as if to warn us, toxic species often have a bitter and sour taste that discourages ingestion. Nonetheless, it's important to be cautious, especially with young children, who may be particularly tempted to taste brightly coloured fruits.

The symptoms observed are primarily digestive in nature: dry mouth, nausea, vomiting, abdominal spasms, and diarrhoea. In some cases, heart or lung complications or even drowsiness and confusion may occur. In these situations, urgent medical care is required. However, such cases are extremely rare.

HYDATID DISEASE

Echinococcosis (hydatid disease) poses the greatest parasite risk from consuming raw fruit. The parasite is most often transmitted by foxes and small forest rodents (occasionally cats and dogs). Eggs are found in solid excrement, not urine, so only fruit soiled by infected faeces can become contaminated.

In humans, the probability of parasitic infection is low and is rare outside mainland Europe, Asia and South America. It occurs mainly in sheep-farming areas. Hotspots in Britain include Powys (and adjacent Herefordshire), Monmouthshire, parts of the Brecon Beacons and the Black Mountains. It is advisable to pick fruit that is higher from the ground, to wash it well, and, as an extra precaution, to cook it above 60°C for several minutes. Cold temperatures, vinegar, and other antiseptics do not kill the parasite. As preventative measures, wear gloves, wash your hands carefully, and administer worming products to cats and dogs.

CONTENTS

This book deals with plant species that produce fleshy fruit.

European barberry, fruit.

IDENTIFICATION KEYS

Correctly identifying plant species can be tricky at times. Depending on the season, the plant's shape and appearance can change. Spring flowers are replaced by autumn berries and stone fruit. Although plants are often easy to identify by examining their flowers, discerning one species from another based on its fruit can prove more difficult, and mistakes are easily made. To make things easier for you, we have compiled a guide to plant parts for the well-informed forager.

General depiction of an inflorescence

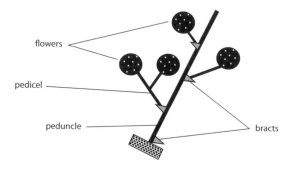

flowers

pedicel

peduncle ── bracts

Depiction of a perfect flower

Note the female reproductive organ, the carpel, and the male reproductive organs, the stamens.

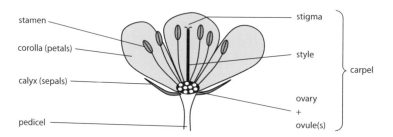

stamen
corolla (petals)
calyx (sepals)
pedicel

stigma
style
ovary
+
ovule(s)

carpel

The parts of a flower can be divided into two broad categories:

- the perianth: consisting of the calyx (sepals) and corolla (petals, in colour, above).
- the reproductive parts: the stamens (collectively known as the androecium) and the carpel(s) (collectively known as the gynoecium).

The sepals, which are generally green and arranged on the outer part of the flower, make up the calyx. Petals are often brightly coloured, positioned inside the flower structure to form the corolla. When petals and sepals are the same colour and shape, they are known as tepals, and together they form the perianth. The arrangement of the flower parts, their symmetry, and the fusing of petals account for the wide variety of shapes formed by the perianth.

The female reproductive organ consists of the carpels. Each carpel is made up of an ovary which contains an ovule, from which projects a small segment (the style) with one or more stigma(s) at the end to receive the pollen. The ovaries can be situated inside or below the perianth. The stamens form the male reproductive system. They can be single or fused, and are sometimes very numerous. Each stamen consists of a small support stalk (the filament) with a pollen-containing structure known as the anther at the top.

Main inflorescence types

The complete flowerhead, which includes the stalks, flowers, and bracts, is known as the inflorescence. The main types are:

Catkin
For example sea grape. A cylindrical collection of small sessile flowers that appear near the bracts.

Raceme
For example redcurrant. A collection of more or less densely packed flowers on a central axis.

Simple corymb
For example common dogwood.
An inflorescence where all the flowers sit in the same plane on pedicels of differing lengths.

Compound corymb
For example rowan.
A collection of small corymbs.

Cyme
For example spindle tree. An arrangement of flowers on short stalks (peduncles) on one side of a central stalk.

Whorl
For example whorled Solomon's seal.
All of the flowers are arranged at same level around a central stem.

Umbel
For example ivy.
The pedicels all emerge from the end of the flower stalk. An umbel is said to be compound when it has a number of individual umbels on a single peduncle.

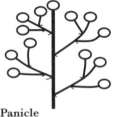

Panicle
For example privet.
A collection of racemes in the shape of a cone.

Spadix
For example water arum. Small sessile flowers on a fleshy body.

Diagram of a simple leaf

A leaf consists of:
- a blade: the large, flat part of the leaf which can take many forms. Leaves can be distinguished by differences in the edges, tips, and bases of their blades.

- a petiole: the shoot that connects the blade to the branch or stalk. It can be short, long, winged, round, flat, or absent (sessile leaf).

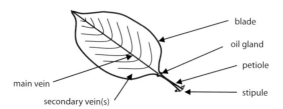

blade

oil gland

petiole

main vein

stipule

secondary vein(s)

Main leaf shapes

Oval, elliptical, lance-shaped, oblong, heart-shaped, needle-shaped ...

Veins run through the leaf blade and can be easily visible or more difficult to discern. They are generally parallel (running parallel for the length of the leaf) in monocotyledons and reticulate (forming a branching network) in dicotyledons. A simple leaf consists of an undivided blade. A compound leaf is made up of a number of blade parts, known as leaflets.

A leaf made up of 7 leaflets (imparipinnate)

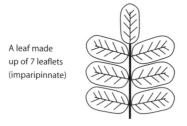

A leaf made up of 6 leaflets (paripinnate)

Most common leaf edge types

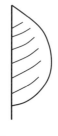

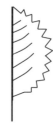

Entire

Crenate

Lobed

Dentate

LEAF TYPES

Main types

Simple leaf

Compound leaves

Needle-shaped leaves

Leaf arrangements

Opposite leaves

Alternate leaves

Whorled leaves

Leaf blade

Entire

Undulate

Lobed

Spiny

Dentate

Crenate

Hairy or downy

Linear

We provide very broad definitions here. Always refer to the standard form of the species in question.

A tree is made up of a number of parts.

The crown of a tree consists of its boughs and lesser branches and its trunk is made up of the tissue between the roots and the crown.

12

Wild Fruit

Herbaceous plants

These plants lack woody lignin. Their aerial parts (stem and leaves) die back each winter. Their height can reach 2 m (for example deadly nightshade), 40–60 cm (for example Solomon's seal), or only 10–20 cm (for example lily of the valley).

Subshrubs

These woody-stemmed plants rarely surpass 1 m in height. Their offshoots remain herbaceous and annual, dying back each year (for example blueberry).

Shrubs

These woody plants, which lack a central trunk, can reach up to 4 m in height. Numerous branches emerge from the soil, giving the plant its bushy (for example rose) or tufted (for example barberry) appearance.

Climbing plants

These pliable-stemmed plants often require supports to grow. They attach themselves with short root-like stems (for example ivy), tendrils (for example grapevine), or by coiling around their support (for example honeysuckle).

Tree-like shrubs

These are up to 7 m tall with a normal, reduced, or nearly non-existent trunk. They can have many branches (for example cornelian cherry) and are often thorny (for example buckthorn). They can also have an adapted shape (for example dwarf whitebeam).

Trees

These woody plants grow to be more than 7 m tall. They have a free-standing trunk that supports the crown of the tree (its branches and leaves). Trees get their rigidity from lignin. Typically, the lower parts of the trunk are free of branches, which can vary from tens of centimetres (for example rowan) to several metres (for example service tree).

Fruit are classed in two broad categories: **fleshy fruit** and **dry fruit**.

The topic of this book being fleshy fruit, we will not concern ourselves with the group of dry fruits, whose membranous carpel tissue remains thin, namely: achenes (chestnut tree, hazelnut tree), capsules (*Datura*), and legumes (laburnums, beans).

Where the carpel tissue is thicker, the fruit is described as fleshy.

We have grouped fleshy fruit in four categories:

Berries
Generally contain several individual seeds arranged in a fleshy envelope (for example common elder, currant).

Drupes
Contain a hard stone that envelops the seed, with a fleshy wall surrounding the stone (for example alder buckthorn, cherry).

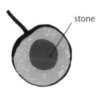

Compound or syncarpous fruits
Formed from tight clusters of mini-drupes known as drupelets (for example raspberry, blackberry).

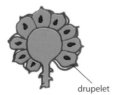

Accessory fruits
A fruit in which some of the flesh comes from tissue at the exterior of the carpel. These include the subgroups hip, of which rose hip is an example, and pome, of which crab apple is an example.

For greater ease of use, we have organized the fleshy fruit species in this book according to the broad categories of plant forms outlined on page 12. Upon finding a plant, the first step is to place it in the right category: herbaceous plant, subshrub, shrub, climbing plant, tree-like shrub, or tree. The colour of the mature fruit also provides a clue to properly identifying the plant. To facilitate this approach, we have given the colour(s) of the fruit in the descriptions of a number of species. For the sake of convenience, each chapter is subdivided according to the type of fruit: berry (for example blueberry), drupe (for example cherry), compound fruit (for example raspberry), and accessory fruit (for example rowan). To complete the identification of each species, we have described the shape and appearance of its flower, accompanied by photographs.

HERBACEOUS PLANTS

These supple plants, which lack the lignin found in woodier species, generally lose their aerial parts in winter. Their size can vary considerably – the result of being highly adapted to their environments – so the group includes the modest lily (20 cm) and majestic deadly nightshade (200 cm). They are organized here according to size: small (smaller than 80 cm) and large (larger than 100 cm), and then by fruit type and colour.

SPECIES	FRUIT	COLOUR	SIZE	PAGE
Arum maculatum	berry	orange-red	small	24
Calla palustris	berry	orange-red	small	25
Convallaria majalis	berry	orange-red	small	26
Maïanthemum bifolium	berry	orange-red	small	27
Physalis alkekengi	berry	orange-red	small	28
Polygonatum verticillatum	berry	orange-red	small	29
Solanum dulcamara	berry	orange-red	small	30
Solanum villosum	berry	orange-red	small	31
Streptopus amplexifolius	berry	orange-red	small	32
Actaea spicata	berry	bluish-black	small	33
Paris quadrifolia	berry	bluish-black	small	34
Polygonatum multiflorum	berry	bluish-black	small	35
Polygonatum odoratum	berry	bluish-black	small	36
Solanum chenopodioides	berry	bluish-black	small	37
Solanum nigrum	berry	bluish-black	small	38

Arisarum vulgare	berry	greenish	small	39
Rubus saxatilis	drupe	orange-red	small	40
Duchesnea indica	accessory fruit	orange-red	small	41
Fragaria vesca	accessory fruit	orange-red	small	42
Iris foetidissima	accessory fruit	orange-red	small	44
Ecballium elaterium	accessory fruit	green	small	45
Asparagus prostratus	berry	orange-red	medium	48
Asparagus officinalis	berry	orange-red	large	46
Atropa belladonna	berry	bluish-black	large	49
Phytolacca decandra (americana)	berry	bluish-black	large	50
Sambucus ebulus	berry	bluish-black	large	51

SUBSHRUBS

These plants rarely exceed 1 m in height. Lacking a central trunk, they are made up of collections of branches that are hard and woody at the base. Their offshoots are herbaceous and die back each winter. They are organized here by fruit type and colour (white, orange-red, or bluish-black).

SPECIES	FRUIT	COLOUR	PAGE
Viscum album	berry	white	54
Daphne alpina	berry	orange-red	55
Daphne cneorum	berry	orange-red	56
Ruscus aculeatus	berry	orange-red	57
Vaccinium oxycoccos	berry	orange-red	58
Vaccinium vitis-idaea	berry	orange-red	59
Empetrum hermaphroditum	berry	bluish-black	60
Vaccinium myrtillus	berry	bluish-black	62
Vaccinium uliginosum	berry	bluish-black	64
Arctostaphylos uva-ursi	drupe	orange-red	65
Osyris alba	drupe	orange-red	66
Ephedra distachya	accessory fruit	orange-red	67
Opuntia ficus-indica	accessory fruit	orange-red	68
Rosa gallica	accessory fruit	orange-red	69
Rubus caesius	compound fruit	bluish-black	70
Cneorum tricoccon	drupaceous dry fruit	orange-red	71

SHRUBS with red fruit

These woody plants, which lack a central trunk, can reach 4 m or more in height. They are made up of many branches that grow out from the roots, and have leaves that may be deciduous or evergreen. They are organized according to fruit type (berry, compound fruit or accessory fruit).

SPECIES	FRUIT	PAGE
Berberis vulgaris	berry	74
Daphne gnidium	berry	75
Daphne mezereum	berry	76
Hypericum androsaemum	berry	77
Lonicera alpigena	berry	78
Lonicera etrusca	berry	79
Lonicera pyrenaica	berry	80
Lonicera xylosteum	berry	81
Lycium barbarum (halimifolium)	berry	82
Pistacia lentiscus	berry	83
Pistacia terebinthus	berry	84
Ribes alpinum	berry	85
Ribes petraeum	berry	86
Ribes rubrum	berry	87
Rubus idaeus	compound fruit	88
Cotoneaster integerrimus	accessory fruit	89
Cotoneaster tomentosus (nebrodensis)	accessory fruit	90
Rosa arvensis	accessory fruit	91
Rosa canina	accessory fruit	92
Rosa foetida	accessory fruit	94
Rosa glauca	accessory fruit	95
Rosa majalis	accessory fruit	96
Rosa pendulina	accessory fruit	97
Rosa rubiginosa	accessory fruit	98
Rosa rugosa	accessory fruit	99
Rosa sempervirens	accessory fruit	100
Rosa tomentosa	accessory fruit	101

Fly honeysuckle, fruit.

SHRUBS with non-red fruit

For the definition of a shrub, see p.16. These shrubs are also organized according to the four fruit types, with the addition of galbulus (round dry fruit that resembles a berry, for example the fruit of *Juniperus sabina*).

SPECIES	FRUIT	COLOUR	PAGE
Asparagus acutifolius	berry	bluish-black	104
Jasminum fruticans	berry	bluish-black	105
Lonicera caerulea	berry	bluish-black	106
Lonicera nigra	berry	bluish-black	107
Lonicera nitida	berry	bluish-black	108
Ribes nigrum	berry	bluish-black	109
Ribes uva-crispa	berry	greenish	110
Symphoricarpos albus	berry	white	111
Daphne laureola	drupe	bluish-black	112
Ligustrum vulgare	drupe	bluish-black	113
Phillyrea angustifolia	drupe	bluish-black	114
Prunus spinosa	drupe	bluish-black	115
Rhamnus alaternus	drupe	reddish black	116
Rhamnus saxatilis	drupe	reddish black	117
Viburnum tinus	drupe	metallic blue	118
Prunus brigantina	drupe	yellow	119
Coriaria myrtifolia	accessory fruit	bluish-black	120
Rosa pimpinellifolia	accessory fruit	bluish-black	121
Rubus fruticosus	compound fruit	bluish-black	122
Juniperus sabina	galbulus	bluish-black	123

CLIMBING PLANTS

These pliable-stemmed plants can grow to be very long and require supports to fully develop. Some species are herbaceous (for example red bryony, black bryony) while others are woody (for example wild grape, common honeysuckle). All of these species produce berries (orange-red, bluish-black, or greenish) except for the blue passion flower (*Passiflora caerulea*), which produces accessory fruit.

SPECIES	FRUIT	COLOUR	PAGE
Bryonia dioica	berry	orange-red	126
Elide asparagoides	berry	orange-red	127

Lonicera caprifolium	berry	orange-red	128
Lonicera implexa	berry	orange-red	129
Lonicera periclymenum	berry	orange-red	130
Smilax aspera	berry	orange-red	131
Tamus communis	berry	orange-red	132
Cucubalus baccifer	berry	bluish-black	133
Hedera helix	berry	bluish-black	134
Parthenocissus tricuspidata	berry	bluish-black	135
Rubia peregrina	berry	bluish-black	136
Vitis vinifera subsp. *sylvestris*	berry	bluish-black	137
Salpichroa origanifolia	berry	yellowish	138
Passiflora caerulea	accessory fruit	orange	139

TREE-LIKE SHRUBS with red, orange, yellow, brown, or greenish fruit

These plants have woody trunks and branches and resemble a small tree. They do not typically exceed 7 m in height. Their trunks are sometimes so short (1–3 cm above ground) that they look like bushes. However, the central axis defined by the trunk in the middle of the branches helps to correctly identify them. In upland areas certain tree-like shrubs adapt to the harsh climate and develop a dwarf form (for example dwarf whitebeam). They are organized here according to fruit type (berry, drupe, or accessory fruit, and for two species, galbulus).

SPECIES	FRUIT	COLOUR	PAGE
Hippophae rhamnoides	berry	orange	142
Arbustus unedo	berry	red	144
Sambucus racemosa	berry	red	145
Cornus mas	drupe	red	146
Elaeagnus multiflora	drupe	red	148
Ilex aquifolium	drupe	red	149
Prunus cerasifera	drupe	red	150
Prunus cerasus	drupe	red	151
Viburnum opulus	drupe	red	152
Prunus dulcis	drupe	greenish	153
Crataegus azarolus	accessory fruit	orange-red	154
Crataegus monogyna	accessory fruit	red	155
Crataegus laevigata	accessory fruit	red	156

Euonymus europaeus	accessory fruit	red	158
Euonymus latifolia	accessory fruit	red	159
Sorbus chamaemespilus	accessory fruit	red	160
Sorbus mougeotii	accessory fruit	red	161
Punica granatum	accessory fruit	brownish-red	162
Cydonia oblonga	accessory fruit	yellowish	163
Malus sylvestris	accessory fruit	yellowish	164
Pyrus spinosa	accessory fruit	brownish-green	165
Pyrus pyraster	accessory fruit	greenish-brown	166
Mespilus germanica	accessory fruit	brownish	168
Juniperus oxycedrus	galbulus	brownish	170
Juniperus phoenicea	galbulus	brownish	171

TREE-LIKE SHRUBS with bluish-black fruit

See the previous definition and notes on organization.

SPECIES	FRUIT	COLOUR	PAGE
Amelanchier ovalis	berry	bluish-black	174
Laurus nobilis	berry	bluish-black	175
Mahonia aquifolium	berry	bluish-black	176
Myrtus communis	berry	bluish-black	177
Sambucus nigra	berry	bluish-black	178
Cornus sanguinea	drupe	bluish-black	180
Frangula alnus	drupe	bluish-black	181
Olea europaea var. sylvestris	drupe	bluish-black	182
Phillyrea latifolia	drupe	bluish-black	183
Prunus domestica subsp. insititia	drupe	bluish-black	184
Prunus laurocerasus	drupe	bluish-black	186
Prunus padus	drupe	bluish-black	187
Rhamnus alpina	drupe	bluish-black	188
Rhamnus catharticus	drupe	bluish-black	189
Rhamnus pumila	drupe	bluish-black	190
Viburnum lantana	drupe	bluish-black	191
Ficus carica	accessory fruit	purple-green	192
Juniperus communis	galbulus	bluish-black	194
Juniperus thurifera	galbulus	bluish-black	193

Briançon apricot, fruit.

Snowy *mespilus*, fruit.

TREES

Trees are defined by their hard trunks and branches, which get their rigidity from lignin, the main component of wood. Adult trees grow to be greater than 7 m in height and the lower part of their trunks is generally free of branches, with a few exceptions (common yew, rowan). The terminal branches that bear the leaves are collectively known as the crown. They are organized here according to fruit type and colour.

SPECIES	FRUIT	COLOUR	PAGE
Diospyros kaki	berry	orange-red	198
Prunus avium	drupe	orange-red	199
Ziziphus zizyphus	drupe	orange-red	200
Celtis australis	drupe	brownish	201
Elaeagnus angustifolia	drupe	brownish	202
Juglans regia	drupe	light green	203
Melia azedarach	drupe	yellowish	204
Prunus serotina	drupe	brownish-black	205
Prunus mahaleb	drupe	bluish-black	206
Morus nigra	compound fruit	bluish-black	207
Sorbus aria	accessory fruit	orange-red	208
Sorbus aucuparia	accessory fruit	orange-red	210
Sorbus domestica	accessory fruit	orange-red	212
Sorbus torminalis	accessory fruit	brownish	213
Sorbus × latifolia	accessory fruit	brownish	214
Taxus baccata	accessory fruit	orange-red	215

Wild cucumber, flowers.

HERBACEOUS PLANTS

These supple plants, which lack the lignin found in woodier species, generally lose their aerial parts in winter. They are very variable in size as a result of being highly adapted to their environments.

Cuckoo pint, normal flower head and cut open.

Italian arum, inflorescence.

LORDS AND LADIES

Arum maculatum · Araceae

Cuckoo pint, fruit.

Lords and ladies, also known as cuckoo pint, has an ingenious system of propagation. The plant gives off a strong, distinctive odour that attracts small flies. Once trapped in a ring of hairs above the flower, the flies remain for several days, during which time they become covered with pollen. On their release, they pollinate the female flowers.

This tuberous perennial herb grows primarily in damp, deciduous forests. Its spearhead-shaped leaves, generally found in pairs, are among the first to appear in spring. They are green, with the upper portion punctuated with dark spots. The leaves are shed after flowering. Its **inflorescence** consists of flowers clustered at the base of its spike-shaped spadix, which is enveloped by a pale green cone-shaped spathe, open at the top. Its **fruit** takes the form of brightly coloured berries, which are grouped together to form an oblong spike. The berries change colour as they ripen, first from green to yellow, then finally to red at maturity.

The leaves and berries are toxic and the leaves can be mistaken for sorrel.

↕	10–30 cm
✴	April/May
🝆	July/September
▲▲	0–1600 m
☠	Toxic

DID YOU KNOW?

Italian arum – *Arum italicum*
Reaching 30 cm in height, this features a yellow flowerhead and spear-shaped leaves with white veins. It bears its fruit late in the season, towards the end of the summer.

∿∿

Water arum, flower.

WATER ARUM

Calla palustris · Araceae

Like the water lily, this perennial plant is found floating on the surface of calm water. Its scientific name derives from the Greek *kallos*, which means beauty. In the rare sites where it does find the right conditions to grow, it propagates extremely quickly. To find it, one must seek out peat bogs, ponds, or acidic marshlands in plains and upland areas. Due to its rarity, it is classed a protected plant in some areas.

The water arum can form large colonies thanks to its creeping rhizomes. Its rounded, heart-shaped green leaves terminate in a small point. The leaves can vary from 6 to 12 cm in length and all originate from the plant's base. The leaves' petioles just break the water's surface. The plant's clustered **flowers** are surrounded by a white spathe that opens rapidly. The inflorescence consists of a small 2–3 cm spike attached to a fleshy axis. Its **fruit** (3–5 mm) take the form of tiny clusters of berries that turn a bright red colour when ripe. The entire plant is poisonous.

Water arum, fruit.

↕	10–30 cm
✳	May/July
⚬⚬	August/September
▲▲	300–800 m
☠	Toxic

Lily of the valley, flowers.

Lily of the valley, leaves and flowers.

LILY OF THE VALLEY

Convallaria majalis · Asparagaceae

Lily of the valley, fruit.

As it is one of the first understorey species to flower, it is perhaps not surprising that the lily of the valley came to be used as an emblem in various ways; in ancient civilizations, it symbolized the return of summer. It is both a common garden plant and one often used by florists. The flowers are said to represent a long-lasting marriage and are often used in bridal bouquets – most famously in that carried by Kate Middleton at her marriage to Prince William. This slender plant, which is also known as May lily, our lady's tears, and May bells, is relatively easy to find.

Lily of the valley sometimes grows in large colonies. Its stem, which sprouts from a spreading rhizome fairly deep below the surface, has purplish-blue scales at the base. The dark green leaves are generally produced in pairs, occasionally in threes; they have nearly parallel veins and are attached to the stalk via long petioles. The small, fragrant, bell-shaped white **flowers** hang to one side of the stem. Its **fruit** takes the form of bright red berries, which, like its flowers, hang from the end of the stem. Like the rest of the plant, they are very toxic – just drinking the water from a glass that held lily of the valley flowers can cause serious health problems.

↕	10–25 cm
✳	End of April/June
⚬⚬	August/October
▲▲	0–1400 m
☠	Toxic

May lily, fruit.

May lily, flowers and leaves.

MAY LILY

Maianthemum bifolium · Asparagaceae

You may sometimes come across sites carpeted with green May lily. This makes it easier to find, as individual plants are spindly and hard to spot. The plant typically has two leaves, though many single-leaved specimens can be found on closer inspection. These single-leaved specimens are sterile and will quickly be eclipsed by other members of the species as flowering time approaches.

May lily is a rhizomatous plant that grows well in light sandy or loamy soil and part shade. It has a frail, angular stem, which bends slightly at the leaf node. The heart-shaped, shiny, alternate leaves have veining that converges to a single point. Varying from pale to dark green, they have a slight undulation along the edge. The small cluster of white upright **flowers**, often in pairs, are at the end of the stem, their four long stamens extending much further than the four tepals. Like the lily of the valley, this plant begins to flower in May. There is a striking resemblance between the two plants, so much so that May lily is often referred to as false lily of the valley. Its **fruit** takes the form of a shiny round berry, 4–5 mm in diameter, mottled with purple spots that turn to a bright red as they age. The berries contain two to six seeds.

May lily, flowers.

↕	15–25 cm
☀	May/June
⬥	July/September
▲▲	200–1700 m
☠	Toxic

Chinese lantern, flowers.

Chinese lantern, flower.

CHINESE LANTERN

Physalis alkekengi · Solanaceae

Chinese lantern, fruit.

This plant's common name comes from its fruit, which resemble brightly coloured paper lanterns. On dreary autumn days, the pods stand out as bright splashes of colour. Inside each one is a flame-red berry.

This herbaceous perennial grows in small colonies. Hairy, angular stems emerge from its creeping roots. The large leaves (12–15 cm) are oval and lance-shaped and attached to the stem by a 5 cm petiole. Single, whitish hanging **flowers** form beneath them. The flower's bell-shaped calyx is made up of five pointed light green sepals, which enclose its five petals; the five stamens are grouped in columns around a single pistil. Its **fruit** takes the form of a bright red berry, surrounded by a red-orange protective film that eventually becomes transparent and fine-meshed. Chinese lantern is rarely found in the wild in Britain.

↕	30–50 cm
☀	May/August
♦♦	September/October
▲▲	0–800 m
▽	Edible but bitter

DID YOU KNOW?

Cape gooseberry – *Physalis peruviana*
This plant has yellow flowers and the edible orange-coloured berries are very rich in vitamin C. It grows along streams and sometimes in urban areas as a garden escape.

～◡

Whorled Solomon's seal, leaves and flowers.

Whorled Solomon's seal, flowers.

Polygonatum verticillatum · Asparagaceae

This alpine species prefers the shade of medium-height shrubs or the forest edge as well as beech woods in upland areas. It is common in Norway and throughout European uplands, for example isolated parts of Scotland, Italy and France, and is often found growing alongside dwarf mountain ash, sorrel and maple. Like its two cousins, Solomon's seal and angular Solomon's seal, its hanging flowers remain half open. However, it is the only one among them with fruit that takes on a purplish-red colour as it ages.

The plant's lumpy rhizome is surrounded by many roots. Its round stem stands erect, bearing long, narrowly lance-shaped leaves which are sessile (lack a petiole). They are arranged in rosettes or whorls at regular intervals along the stem. Small clusters of **flowers** droop from the upper leaf whorls, their green-white tepals forming an open-ended tube. There is a small bract on each peduncle that attaches the flower to the stalk. The **fruit** are the size of a small pea and take the form of berries that change colour from green to crimson mottled with black, then finally to a violet-red at maturity. They remain on the plant long after it has shed its leaves.

Whorled Solomon's seal, fruit.

↕	40–80 cm
☀	May/July
⚭	Mid-August/September
▲▲	700–2000 m
☠	Toxic

Herbaceous Plants

Woody nightshade, flowers.

WOODY NIGHTSHADE

Solanum dulcamara · Solanaceae

Woody nightshade, fruit.

The sweet flavour of this plant's leaves quickly gives way to an unpleasant and extremely bitter taste when they are chewed. These disparate flavours are caused by two substances from the same family of molecules: saponins. The first sweet-flavoured substance is detected quickly, while the second, with its bitter taste, takes longer to reveal itself. The plant's scientific name *dulcamara*, which literally means 'sweet-bitter', refers to this phenomenon. It is also called bittersweet and poisonberry.

Often woody at its base, woody nightshade develops long, angular, hanging stems which frequently intermingle with neighbouring species. Its lance-shaped, slightly hairy, alternate leaves are sometimes divided into three unequal lobes (a large lobe above the two smaller lateral lobes). Its **flowers**, whose purple petals contrast sharply with the yellow anthers of its stamens, form small loose cymes. The plant's **fruit** takes the form of egg-shaped berries, which change from green to yellow to scarlet red as they ripen. The berries are about the size of a pea and contain many seeds. The berries are most toxic when green.

↕	0.5–2 m
☀	May/October
🍒	August/November
🌰	0–1800 m
☠	Toxic

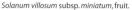
Solanum villosum subsp. miniatum, fruit.

Red nightshade, flowers.

Solanum villosum · Solanaceae

The plant's genus, *Solanum*, contains the Latin root *sol*, which means 'sun'. This suggests some sort of special connection with the sun. Many of its species do thrive in the sun's heat, without which they could not reach full maturity. Not usually found in Britain.

Red nightshade, also known as woolly nightshade, is made up of slightly angular drooping branches. A dense coat of whitish hairs covers the plant. Its oval, entire leaves have roughly dentate edges and large, hairy petioles. Its white **flowers**, which have yellow anthers and hairy calyces and pedicels, form small clusters. The **fruit**, which are poisonous, take the form of nearly round, shiny, orange-yellow berries, 6–10 mm in diameter, resembling small cherry tomatoes and containing large numbers of seeds. As with tomatoes, the remains of the flower's calyx stays attached to the fruit. Though it is quite a rare plant, red nightshade can be found along roadways, in fields, and around the ruins of old buildings.

Red nightshade, fruit.

DID YOU KNOW?
Solanum villosum subsp. *miniatum* has small wing-like branches covered in small hairs.

〜〰

↕	30–60 cm
☀	June/September
⬦⬦	August/October
⛰	200–1000 m
☠	Toxic

Herbaceous Plants

Wild cucumber, flowers.

WILD CUCUMBER

Streptopus amplexifolius · Liliaceae

Wild cucumber, fruit.

Wild cucumber, fruit.

This is a curious plant. Its scientific name comes from the Greek *streptos*, which means 'to bend', and *podos*, 'foot'. The fruit are suspended on thin twisted peduncles beneath the leaves, and it is from this feature it derives its other common name, clasping twistedstalk. It grows in damp, shady habitats, such as beech woods and mossy rock outcrops throughout Britain and Europe. A very rare plant, it is a protected species in many regions.

The plant grows from a small rhizome which has many roots. Its round, branched stem, which curves alternately in opposite directions, becomes more angular at the top of the plant. Its oval, alternate leaves lack petioles and seem to completely embrace the stalk; they have thick veins that converge at the base. The plant's lone **flowers** hang beneath the leaves on long, thin filaments that bend downwards. The six whitish tepals (8–10 mm) are fused at the base of the flower and curved at the ends; inside are six stamens. Its **fruit** are long scarlet red berries (10–12 mm), which hang on long, thin peduncles. They contain a number of grey seeds. Although cows feed on it, its toxicity is not yet fully understood, so exercise caution.

↕	50–80 cm
✳	May/mid-August
🍒	July/September
⛰	800–2000 m
☠	Toxic

Red baneberry, flowers.

RED BANEBERRY

Actaea spicata · Ranunculaceae

This perennial herb is most often found on chalky soil in damp habitats or at the foot of hills. Though the fresh plant causes irritation when touched, its dried leaves were once used to treat certain skin problems. They were ground into a powder to form the base for a preparation used against fleas, mites, and ticks. Also known as snakeberry, today it is often used as a homeopathic remedy.

Attached to the plant's branched stem are 2–3 sizeable leaves, each of which is made up of roughly dentate leaflets. Its tiny white **flowers**, which are arranged in short, dense terminal or axillary (at the upper angle of where the leaf stalk meets the stem) clusters, give off a rather unpleasant odour. The plant sheds its petals and its tiny sepals surround a number of slender whitish stamens. Its toxic **fruit** takes the form of berries, 5–7 mm in diameter, which turn from green to black as they mature and contain many seeds.

Red baneberry, fruit.

↕	40–70 cm
☀	May/July
🝆	July/September
▲▲	200–1600 m
☣	Toxic

Herb paris, leaves and flower.

Herb paris, seven-leaved seedling.

HERB PARIS

Paris quadrifolia · Melanthiaceae

Herb paris, fruit.

In Latin, *paris* means 'equal', which alludes to the perfectly symmetrical leaves that adorn the plant. It is also known as true lover's knot and devil-in-a-bush.

Herb paris grows in colonies, sometimes of considerable size. Its preferred habitats include the undergrowth and damp and shady areas. The leaves are at the end of its stem, arranged in a rosette. They are sessile and oval, tapering to a small point, and the veins make an easily visible network on their surface. There is a single **flower** per stem, 2–3 cm above the leaves, which consists of four broad green sepals and four narrow yellow-green petals, topped with 8–12 yellowish stamens. Its solitary bluish-black **fruit**, on top of the stem, can exceed 1.5 cm in diameter and contains dark brown seeds.

↕	10–30 cm
☀	May/August
⚭	July/October
⛰	100–2000 m
☠	Toxic

DID YOU KNOW?

Five-leaved specimens are sometimes observed. Even rarer are six-leaved specimens and rarest of all are the seven-leaved.

∾

Polygonatum multiflorum subsp. *bracteatum*, stems, leaves, and flowers.

Solomon's seal, flowers.

SOLOMON'S SEAL

Polygonatum multiflorum · Asparagaceae

Often clustered in imposing colonies, these plants suggest soldiers on parade because of their tendency to orient themselves in the same direction. There are a number of explanations for the names. On the rhizome, once the stem has dried out after the growing season, a prominent circular scar that resembles a seal appears. On the surface of the rhizome, a number of bumps that bear an uncanny resemblance to knees are visible. These 'many knees', gave the genus its name: Polygonatum, from the Greek *poly*, meaning 'many', and *gony*, 'knees'.

The stem of Solomon's seal is round, smooth, and curved in the leaved areas. Its large, oval, nearly sessile leaves are arranged alternating in two rows. Its **flowers**, borne in hanging clusters, consist of whitish tepals with six small greenish lobes at their end, which form a tube with an opening at the end. Its **fruit** takes the form of dark blue berries made up of three sections. It is often found in the shade, in damp wooded areas.

Solomon's seal, fruit.

↕	20–50 cm
☀	May/June
🝙	August/Mid-October
⛰	0–1700 m
☠	Toxic

Herbaceous Plants

Hybrid of *Polygonatum multiflorum* and *Polygonatum odoratum*.

Angular Solomon's seal, flowers.

ANGULAR SOLOMON'S SEAL

Polygonatum odoratum · Asparagaceae

Angular Solomon's Seal, fruit.

This lovely plant that inhabits the forest edge and undergrowth was once used medicinally – its rhizome was said to have healing and anti-rheumatic properties and even the ability to treat gout. Today, it is no longer used for medicinal purposes. The plant is capable of hybridizing with Solomon's seal (*Polygonatum multiflorum*), which sometimes results in specimens with stems that are much taller than those of its parents.

The plant's square stem bends upwards. Its oval, sessile, alternate leaves are arranged in two rows. At the centre of the leaves, prominent parallel veins are visible. Its **flowers**, which are slightly fragrant, are found individually or in pairs just above where the leaves meet the stem. The tepals form a long white tube (1.5–2 cm) with an opening at the end and six stamens hang from short peduncles. Its **fruit** takes the form of spherical bluish-black berries, 8–10 mm in diameter, covered with bloom (a powdery coating that gives them a frosted appearance). This common species is often found in partially shaded areas and prefers chalky soil.

↕	20–40 cm
✳	April/July
◊◊	August/September
▲▲	0–1800 m
✸	Toxic

DID YOU KNOW?
Polygonatum multiflorum × *odoratum*
This hybrid results from the crossing of two species of blue-fruited Solomon's seal.

～ノ

Green nightshade.   Leafy-fruited nightshade.   Velvety nightshade, flowers.

VELVETY NIGHTSHADE

Solanum chenopodioides · Solanaceae

This plant, also known as petty morel, is easily mistaken for the more common black nightshade, but on closer inspection it reveals some identifying features. Plants of the genus *Solanum* are full of surprises; the colour of the fruit is variable, as is the shape of the leaves and the appearance of the downy hairs that cover the stems and leaves.

The stem of velvety nightshade has slender branches and is woody at its base. The whole plant is covered in short hairs and the leaves are entire. Its **flowers** are about 1 cm in size and are borne in clusters of 3–5 to form a small cyme. The calyx consists of triangular sepals and the white petals are arranged in a star shape. Its **fruit** is a matt black berry.

Velvety nightshade, fruit.

DID YOU KNOW?

The rarest nightshades are:
S. nitidibaccatum (green nightshade),
S. triflorum (cutleaf nightshade),
S. sarachoides (leafy-fruited nightshade).

↕	20–50 cm
✳	May/October
🍒	August/November
⛰	0–600 m
☠	Toxic

Herbaceous Plants

Black nightshade, flowers.

Black nightshade, dentate-leaved variety.

BLACK NIGHTSHADE

Solanum nigrum · Solanaceae

Black nightshade, fruit.

Black nightshade, yellow-fruited variety.

DID YOU KNOW?

S. nigrum var. *chlorocarpum* is yellow-fruited.
S. nigrum var. *atriplicifolium* is dentate-leaved.

~~~

↕	30–80 cm
☀	June/September
⚘	August/October
⛰	0–1000 m
☠	Toxic

Common along the edges of freshly ploughed fields, black nightshade (also known as hound nightshade and garden nightshade) is noted for its ability to attract and kill certain insects. It is therefore planted with potato crops to control potato beetles. Datura and castor oil plants can also be used for this purpose, but unfortunately all of these plants are equally toxic to humans.

The plant's main stem subdivides into a number of angular branches, which are covered in rough hairs. Its simple alternate leaves are oval to lance-shaped with a wavy leaf edge. It has a thick, long (3–4 cm), hairy stem. Its small **flowers**, which are made up of a calyx consisting of five rounded lobes and a larger white star-shaped corolla, cluster together to form cymes. Its stamens have long anthers gathered together in a compact yellow tube, from which the stigma emerges. The plant's **fruit** takes the form of spherical berries (8–10 mm) that change colour from green to black. The mature berries can be found coexisting alongside flowers on the same plant. The dried remains of the sepals are visible at the base of the berries, which form small hanging clusters. They contain a purplish-black juice and a very large number of small hard seeds known as pips, and are most toxic when green. A very common plant throughout Europe, it prefers light soils, such as those bordering fields, flowerbeds, or uncultivated land.

Friar's cowl, fruit and inflorescences.

FRIAR'S COWL

Arisarum vulgare · Araceae

This is a relatively rare plant, which is primarily native to the Mediterranean region and is not found in Britain. The inflorescence resembles a hood or cloak, from which comes the name friar's cowl. It thrives along roadsides and on uncultivated scrubland. Wild boars are very fond of its edible tubers, and it is not uncommon to find sites where the soil seems to have been ploughed in their quest to track them down. Historically, the plant's tubers were dried and made into flour during periods of famine.

Its long stem, which is punctuated with purple spots, grows from a large oval tuber. The spearhead-shaped leaves, which can grow to 8 cm in length, have two divergent lobes at their base and are attached to the stem by long spotted petioles. It has an unusual **inflorescence**, unique to the genus *Arum*. The flower's large bract forms a long sheath, known as a spathe, that encloses the inflorescence. The lower part of the bract takes the form of a green and white striped tube, while its upper part is mauve in colour and shaped like curved cowl. A cylindrical green spadix (a spike of tiny, closely arranged flowers), in the form of a club that curves towards the front, extends beyond the bract by several millimetres. Its **fruit** takes the form of cube-shaped greenish berries, clustered at the end of the stem.

Friar's cowl, inflorescence.

↕	10–30 cm
✳	March/April and October/November
♣	April/May and November/December
▲▲	0–400 m
☠	All parts are toxic except the tuber

Stone bramble, flowers.

STONE BRAMBLE

Rubus saxatilis · Rosaceae

Stone bramble, fruit.

Unlike most other brambles, which are shrubs, the stone bramble is herbaceous. This rather inconspicuous plant is often confused with the more common alpine strawberry, as a result of its similar leaves. Its nectar is a favourite among pollinating insects. It grows at a wide range of altitudes, from plains to upland areas, but is rare in Britain except for northern England and Scotland.

This small perennial herb's tiny prickles are so fine they are barely visible to the naked eye. Each leaf is made up of three oval leaflets, of which only the terminal leaflet has a petiole. They are light green on both sides and roughly dentate. The flowering stems stand erect and the **flowers**, which have a calyx of more or less erect sepals and a corolla made up of thin white petals, are grouped in tiny corymbs. The flower's stamens extend farther than its style. The **fruit** is an aggregate of small, shiny, translucent, bright red drupes. They ripen towards the end of summer, but have a rather bland flavour.

	20–25 cm
✳	May/June
🍒	July/September
▲▲	200–2300 m
👄	Edible

Wild Fruit

Mock strawberry, flower.

MOCK STRAWBERRY

Potentilla indica · Rosaceae

This species originated in India and was first used in gardens as groundcover or border edging. It quickly spread from gardens into the wild, its dispersal achieved by the ants and birds that are very fond of its seeds. The mock strawberry is often used as a groundcover plant in edible forest gardens. The fruit is a vivid red and looks as delicious as a true strawberry, but has a rather insipid taste which can leave you feeling a little cheated. It grows in the grounds of Wells Cathedral.

The mock strawberry's long creeping stems, or stolons, can reach up to 80 cm in length, which is one way to distinguish it from the alpine strawberry. Its leaves, which are at regular intervals along the stem, are divided into three leaflets with dentate edges. Supported by a long peduncle, its single **flower** has five bright yellow petals. The calyx is lined with five large three-toothed sepals forming a second calyx, known as the calycule. Resembling a strawberry in colour and shape and 2–3 cm in diameter, its **fruit** contain multiple achenes (fruit containing the seed) and have little flavour.

Mock strawberry, fruit.

↕	10–15 cm
✳	May/September
🍒	July/October
▲▲	0–1000 m
✂	Inedible

Alpine strawberry, flowers.

ALPINE STRAWBERRY

Fragaria vesca · Rosaceae

Alpine strawberry, fruit.

This perennial plant has a lovely fragrance. Its diminutive size means that passers-by often miss the chance to pick large quantities of its berries, which are rich in vitamins and trace elements. As they pack a high water content and are not overly sweet, they make for an effective thirst-quencher.

The leaf stalks of alpine strawberry are shorter than the flower stalks. Each leaf is divided into three large-toothed leaflets, shinier on top and dark green and slightly silky to the touch on the undersurface. The white **flowers** (10–15 mm) are formed of overlapping petals and clearly separated sepals. Bracts are sometimes present on its floral stems. The semispherical **fruit** is easily detached from the plant. It is covered in achenes (small dry fruit that contain the seed) of varying shades of red. Large colonies of the plant can be found in freshly felled areas of woodland, particularly in sunnier spots.

↕	10–25 cm
✳	May/August
🍒	June/September
⛰	0–1500 m
👄	Edible

DID YOU KNOW?

Green strawberry – *Fragaria viridis*
The plant's fairly large, whitish flowers (16–20 mm) have tight petals. The sepals remain on the fruit, which is difficult to detach from the plant.

Hautbois strawberry – *Fragaria moschata*
These plants grow to be 30–40 cm tall. Runners are few or non-existent on this species. Its fruit is inedible.

∿

Green strawberry, flowers.

Green strawberry, fruit.

Hautbois strawberry, leaflets.

RECIPE

ALPINE STRAWBERRY WINE

Ingredients
250 g alpine strawberries
500 ml unflavoured or raspberry-flavoured spirits
500 ml sweet white wine

Method
Pass the strawberries through a food mill. Place the pulp in a large jar and add
the spirits and wine. Allow to steep for three weeks.
Filter the mixture through a muslin cloth. Allow it to settle for 48 hours and
decant the clear liquid. The wine is now ready to drink. Serve cold.

Stinking iris, flowers.

Stinking iris, leaves and fruit.

STINKING IRIS

Iris foetidissima · Iridaceae

This iris is prized for its decorative seeds that last well into winter, which is why it is often found in ornamental gardens. It gets its name from the fact that its leaves give off a rather unpleasant odour when bruised.

The plant features several long sword-shaped leaves and a flowering stem, growing from a rhizome. Two or three bluish **flowers** made up of six long, purple-veined tepals are borne at the end of the stem. The outer tepals spread out, while the inner ones stand upright. The egg-shaped **fruit** capsule turns from green to a brownish colour, and eventually opens up into three parts to reveal the seeds, carried in two rows. Resembling berries because of their bright red colour, they are of little interest to birds and thus often remain untouched. The red pigment they contain was once widely used to dye cloth.

Stinking iris, fruit.

↕	25–60 cm
✳	May/July
🍒	September
▲▲	0–600 m
✶	Toxic

Squirting cucumber, flowers and fruit.

Ecballium elaterium · Cucurbitaceae

The plant's various names, which also include exploding cucumber, paint a vivid picture of the species' unusual characteristics. Children love to watch it shoot out its seeds over long distances, not unlike a catapult. Be careful not to direct it towards the face, however, as a great deal of pressure builds up inside the mature fruit – its numerous seeds are projected in a tenth of a second. The species favours abandoned urban spaces, roadsides, and fallow land, where it forms small creeping colonies. It grows in temperate mainland Europe but is absent from Britain.

Covered in short, stiff hairs, its strong stems support thick, triangular, hairy leaves, which are whitish on the underside and greenish on top. The edges are irregularly lobed or coarsely toothed and undulating. Male and female **flowers** grow on the same plant, the male flowers forming tight clusters that grow out from just above where the leaf stalk meets the stem, while the female flowers are single. The lance-shaped calyx is topped with a corolla made up of yellowish veined petals. The **fruit** takes the form of a greenish, medium-sized, oblong berry, which is striped along its length and rough to the touch. The berries contain many brown seeds.

Squirting cucumber, fruit.

↕	20–80 cm
✳	March/September
🍒	June/November
▲▲	0–300 m
🥀	Inedible

Narrow-leaved asparagus, fruit.

Narrow-leaved asparagus, flowers.

GARDEN ASPARAGUS

Asparagus officinalis · Asparagaceae

Garden asparagus, spear.

Asparagus derives its name from the Persian word *asparag*, meaning 'to sprout' or 'spring up'. Colloquially, this became 'sparrow-grass', a name which persisted until the last century. The species is found sporadically in areas with sandy soil, on roadsides, and along the perimeter of fields; it grows wild in areas of Bristol, England. It is rarely encountered on higher ground. The plant is widely cultivated and consumed throughout Europe.

The underground parts of garden asparagus are known as the crown. It is the year's young shoots or spears, with their sweet flavour, that are harvested for food. The plant develops a number of branching shoots that bear needle-like modified stems known as cladodes in clusters of up to ten. It produces greenish dioecious **flowers** (the male and female flowers on separate plants) in the shape of small, elongated bells, found individually or in pairs. The **fruit** are round berries, which change from green to a brownish colour, then to a shiny red as they age. The berries contain 3–4 black seeds and are toxic.

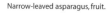

↕	0.8–1.2 m
✳	June/July
◊◊	Mid-August/October
▲▲	0–700 m
🐝	Fruit: toxic
👄	Spears: edible

DID YOU KNOW?

Narrow-leaved asparagus – *Asparagus tenuifolius*
The plant's long needles (cladodes) are whorled in groups of 10–25.
The plant's fruit is the size of a cherry.

∿

Garden asparagus, male flower.

Garden asparagus, female flower.

Garden asparagus, fruit.

Wild asparagus, flowers.

Asparagus maritimus, flowers.

WILD ASPARAGUS

Asparagus officinalis subsp. *prostratus* · Asparagaceae

Wild asparagus, fruit.

This inconspicuous species can be found under the shelter of maritime pines and on or between sand dunes in mainland Europe. The plant has adapted to this coastal environment by developing strong underground roots and is not disturbed by the strong winds; its growth is unaffected by being covered in sand.

The prostrate, usually curving stems produce short alternating branches that are either creeping or barely raised above the ground. They bear small (5–7 cm), thick, stiff, leathery cladodes (leaf-like modified stems), which are bluish green in colour and carried in clusters. The yellowish **flowers**, found individually or in pairs, grow out from just above where the branches meet the stem. The flowers hang on short peduncles and are shaped like little cowbells. Its **fruit** takes the form of round berries, which change from orange to red as they ripen and feature a tiny barb on the end.

↕	20–60 cm
☀	May/July
⚭	August/September
⛰	0–100 m
☣	Toxic (fruit)

DID YOU KNOW?

Asparagus maritimus
This plant can reach 1 m in height and its cladodes are rough to the touch. It is mainly found in the Mediterranean region.

～～

Yellow belladonna, fruit.

Deadly nightshade, flower.

DEADLY NIGHTSHADE

Atropa belladonna · Solanaceae

Deadly nightshade, fruit.

Deadly nightshade seems designed to please, the shape and colour of its flowers and its shiny, enticing berries all conspiring to attract attention. Although it is also known as love apple, its other common names – devil's herb, witch's berry and sorcerer's cherry – suggest something more sinister. The differing accounts of the plant derive from the ways in which it is used. In small doses, applied as an ointment around the eyes, it causes the pupils to dilate, while in larger doses it is deadly. This contradiction is reflected in its scientific name, which refers to *belladonna*, or 'beautiful lady', and Atropos, the Ancient Greek goddess responsible for cutting the thread of life.

The plant thrives in chalky soil, where it can be found in large numbers, preferring open areas such as clearings, felled woodland and roadsides. The upper part of its robust stem is branched. It has oval, entire leaves which are found in pairs (one larger and one smaller) at the end of its stems. The leaves on the lower parts of the stem are alternate. Borne singly or in pairs, its purplish-pink **flowers** are shaped like a small bell with a hairy calyx which is divided into five lobes that taper to a point. Its **fruit** takes the form of shiny berries, which change from green to black as they ripen. The berries are very toxic, as is the rest of the plant. A few berries are enough to cause a very serious case of poisoning.

DID YOU KNOW?
Yellow belladonna – *Atropa belladonna* var. *lutea* This variety has fruit that are yellowish in colour.

↕	0.7–1.4 m
☀	June/August
◔◔	August/October
▲▲	0–1500 m
☠	Toxic

Poke root, fruit.

Poke root, flowers.

POKE ROOT

Phytolacca decandra · Phytolaccaceae

Phytolacca esculenta, fruit.

Poke root is an invasive species which is classed as a plant pest as it forms large colonies that overtake other species of flowering plants and deplete the soil of humus. The result is that soil becomes less fertile and biodiversity diminishes. The only means of eradicating it is to completely destroy the plants, which are found on uncultivated land and along roadsides.

Poke root's tall, purple-tinged stem carries symmetrical branches. Its large (25–30 cm), undulate, alternate leaves are oval, tapering to a point, and are attached to the stalk by a short petiole. The plant produces several clusters of slightly curved **flowers**, which turn from an initial greenish shade to pink. The corolla is made up of five petals, ten stamens and ten styles. Its ripe **fruit** takes the form of shiny black berries that hang from the stalk, the remains of the flower parts discernible in the small depressions at the end of the berries. They are made up of ten small chambers, each containing a single seed suspended in black inky juice.

↕	1.5–3.5 m
✳	July/September
🍒	August/October
⛰	0–700 m
☠	Somewhat toxic

DID YOU KNOW?

Phytolacca esculenta
The plant's flowers and fruit are arranged in upright clusters. Each fruit is made up of eight chambers.

∽

Dwarf elder, flowers.

DWARF ELDER

Sambucus ebulus · Caprifoliaceae

Dwarf elder is a frequent cause of poisoning among adults, since its small clusters of black fruit resemble common elderberries. While dwarf elder is herbaceous with berries on erect stalks and common elder is a shrub with hanging berries, the two species are sometimes found growing next to each other, the lower branches of the latter intermingling with the upper herbaceous stalks of the former.

Forming large colonies, dwarf elder is often found in sunny or partially shaded areas and prefers chalky soil. Its longitudinally striated stems stand straight and upright and contain a whitish pith inside. The very large, opposite leaves are made up of 7–9 long, lance-shaped, finely dentate leaflets. Its **flowers**, which consist of white petals and purplish-red anthers, are borne in imposing, branched corymbs, and give off an unusual aroma. The **fruit** takes the form of round, shiny, black berries that form large clusters at the end of an upright stem. Accidental ingestion can causes serious digestive symptoms.

Dwarf elder, fruit.

↕	1–1.5 m
☀	June/September
⚬⚬	August/October
⛰	0–1500 m
☠	Toxic

Herbaceous plants

Alpine daphne, fruit.

SUBSHRUBS

These plants rarely surpass 1 m in height. Lacking a central trunk, they have woody overwintering stems with herbaceous summer growth.

Mistletoe, male flower.

Mistletoe, female flower.

Mistletoe, fruit.

Pine mistletoe, fruit.

MISTLETOE

Viscum album · Loranthaceae

Spruce mistletoe, fruit.

Because of its association with Christmas, mistletoe is most familiar as a festive decoration. It is also known as all-heal. This plant is a hemi-parasite, or partial parasite, which means that it obtains water and nutrients from its host but is also capable of photosynthesis. It attaches to its host (often an apple tree or hawthorn, occasionally oak or elm) by means of a modified root called a haustorium, which causes damage to the wood. Its round, fragile, branched stems with their greenish bark form a round clump.

The thick, 3–7 cm long, strap-shaped, sessile leaves are in opposite pairs. They are leathery textured, with the veins barely visible. The yellowish male and female **flowers**, which are found on different stalks, lack pedicels and form small clusters. The flower's perianth is made up of four tepals. Its **fruit** – whitish, round berries (6–10 mm) – contain a viscous pulp and seeds. The berries can remain on the branches for as long as two years.

↕	40–50 cm
☀	March/May
◗◗	Mid-November/February
▲▲	0–1300 m
☠	Toxic

DID YOU KNOW?

Spruce mistletoe – *Viscum album* subsp. *abietis*
This plant's green seeds are surrounded by a network of whitish mesh. It grows only on spruce trees (*Abies*).

Pine mistletoe – *Viscum album* subsp. *austriacum*
The fruit of this species are slightly yellower. It is only found on Scots pine (*Pinus*) and larch trees (*Larix*).

෨෴

Alpine daphne, flowers.

Daphne alpina · Thymelaeaceae

This plant is named after the Ancient Greek nymph Daphne, said to have been Apollo's first love. The story goes that she was pursued by Apollo after refusing to speak to him. Before she was caught, she begged her father, the river god Ladon, for help, and he transformed her into a laurel. Apollo consoled himself by designating the laurel his sacred tree.

Alpine daphne grows in well-exposed rocky or stony soil and even in rocky crevices in southern and central Europe. Its knotty, winding main stem divides into a number of branches which are covered with soft hair. Long (2–4 cm), lance-shaped, hairy leaves form a rosette at the end of its stems. Clusters of white **flowers**, which give off a subtle aroma, are borne at the very ends of the branches. Each flower is made up of four small petals in a cross shape. The **fruit** takes the form of 4–6 mm, oblong orange berries, which contain a single seed. The young berries are downy and become smooth as they ripen. Like the rest of the plant, they are toxic.

Alpine daphne, fruit.

↕	50–80 cm
☀	April–May
🍒	July/August
❄	400–2000 m
	Toxic

Garland flower, flowers.

GARLAND FLOWER

Daphne cneorum · Thymelaeaceae

Striated daphne, flowers.

The garland flower and striated daphne (*Daphne striata*) are nearly identical in appearance – the few small details that differentiate them can be discerned only on close inspection. Both are rare plants, and to find a specimen in fruit is a rare privilege, as the fruiting is brief and occasional. When they are in bloom, the strong fragrance of the flowers is hard to miss.

This subshrub prefers the chalky and stony soil of pine forests, undergrowth, and sunny forest edges. Its many stems divide into small hairy branches which bear the 2–3 cm long, sessile evergreen leaves in clusters at the ends. Large numbers of fragrant, lilac-scented, light pink to purplish-pink **flowers** form dense clusters. The flower's calyx is covered with short soft hairs. The **fruit** takes the form of egg-shaped, orange berries, 5–6 mm in diameter, which are attached directly to the stalk. The berries remain on the plant for a very short period of time.

↕	15–30 cm
☀	April/May
♦♦	Extremely rare, July/August
▲▲	200–2000 m
🐛	Toxic

DID YOU KNOW?

Striated daphne – *Daphne striata*
This plant has hairless branches and grows to a height 5–20 cm. Its leaves are narrower and more elongated in their terminal bundles. The flower's calyx has hairless sepals and its fruit are orange-red. These rare plants are found on grasslands at higher altitudes. Like all daphnes, it is toxic.

Wild Fruit

Butcher's broom, male flowers.

Butcher's broom, female flowers.

Butcher's broom, fruit.

Butcher's broom, young shoots.

Ruscus aculeatus · Asparagaceae

Commonly used medicinally for its circulation-enhancing properties, this plant has other virtues – its young shoots are delicious served either raw or cooked and the robust, flat, thorny branches can be used in all manner of Christmas decorations.

This clump-forming evergreen subshrub favours warm or partially shaded habitats in sparsely wooded areas, dry heaths and hedges. It has dense, straight branches, which are vertically striped and bear pseudo-leaves known as cladophylls. Dark green and tapering to a fine point, these are generally no longer than 3 cm. Its discreet **flowers**, which are greenish-white with a purple tinge, grow from the centre of the cladophylls. The plant produces nearly round, shiny, bright red **fruit** which are 1 cm in diameter and remain on the plant for a long period of time. Each contains one or two seeds.

Horse tongue lily, flower.

Spineless butcher's broom, fruits.

DID YOU KNOW?

Horse tongue lily – *Ruscus hypoglossum*
A large spur emerges from the middle of the plant's cladophyll, beneath which the flower is borne.

Spineless butcher's broom – *Ruscus hypophyllum*
The plant's large cladophylls sit close together. It is found in rocky shaded areas.

~~

↕	30–70 cm
✺	September/April
⬢⬢	Almost year-round
⛰	0–700 m
🍒	Fruit: toxic
👄	Young shoots: edible but bitter

Subshrubs

Bog cranberry, flower.

American cranberry, fruit.

Small cranberry, flowers.

BOG CRANBERRY

Vaccinium oxycoccos · Ericaceae

Bog cranberry, fruit.

The bog cranberry, also known by the botanical name *Oxycoccus palustris*, is protected in some parts of Europe. The sparse populations are most often found at high altitudes in bogs and marshes, hence the common names bog cranberry and marsh cranberry. The American cranberry or large cranberry, which is currently enjoying much popularity, is abundant in the marshes of northern Europe and America, where it is mechanically harvested.

Bog cranberry forms creeping clumps of thin, flexible stems, which root at the nodes. The leathery, 5–8 mm long oval leaves are shiny on top and roll inwards at the edges. It produces **flowers** in groups of three or four, attached to the stem by long, fine pedicels covered in small downy hairs. The flower's light pink corolla is made up of four petals which fold back on themselves. Its **fruit** takes the form of round berries (15–20 mm) that are yellow at first, mottled with darker spots, and become dark red as they mature. The berries ripen in September and have a somewhat sour flavour.

DID YOU KNOW?

Small cranberry – *Vaccinium microcarpum*
The plant's triangular leaves are straight at the base of the leaf blade. Its pedicels and petioles lack downy hairs and the fruit are smaller.

American cranberry – *Vaccinium macrocarpon*
This species has oblong leaves and its fruit can measure up to 2 cm in diameter.

↕	10–30 cm
☀	May/Mid-August
🍒	September/October
▲▲	100–2100 m
👄	Edible

Cowberry, flowers.

Cowberry, fruit.

Vaccinium vitis-idaea · Ericaceae

The berries of this plant are a favourite in the kitchen as they make exquisite jellies and jams, which can be served as an accompaniment to meat, game and fish. They have a bitter flavour and are a source of vitamin A, vitamin C, and a number of trace elements. According to some connoisseurs, it is best to pick the berries before the first frost in order to better preserve their flavour.

The tips of the plant's young green, angular creeping shoots stand upright. The small, leathery, oval, entire leaves are marked with dark spots and are slightly rolled in on themselves, with a small indentation at their tips. Clusters of pinkish, cowbell-shaped **flowers** (6–9 mm) hang from the ends of the stems. The **fruit** takes the form of round, bright red berries that form small clusters, standing out against the green leaves. The berries are less than 1 cm in diameter and contain slightly acidic white flesh, which makes them unpalatable when raw. The species is often confused with bearberry.

RECIPE

COWBERRY COMPOTE

Ingredients
500 g freshly picked cowberries
250 g caster sugar
250 ml water

Method
Wash the berries well and allow to drain. Combine the water and sugar in a pan and heat to a boil. Allow the syrup to cool for one minute and add the fruit. Cook on low heat until the berries burst, about 15–20 minutes. Pass the mixture through a food mill with a fine sieve to obtain a smooth texture.

Uses
This compote is traditionally served as an accompaniment to wild game and poultry. It can also be used as a topping on bread or rice cakes. It freezes well.

↕	20–25 cm
☀	June/August
🍒	September/ October
⛰	200–3000 m
👄	Edible

Subshrubs

Mountain crowberry, leaves.

MOUNTAIN CROWBERRY

Empetrum nigrum subsp. *hermaphroditum* · Empetraceae

Mountain crowberry, fruit.

Found mainly in alpine habitats and upland areas of Scotland, this plant requires very specific conditions to grow: reasonably acidic soil, sufficient humidity throughout the year and a cool climate. It is therefore mainly limited to bogs, boggy heaths, and damp rocky slopes where snow accumulates and helps to keep the soil moist. In Nordic countries it is prepared as tea, which has a sour, peppery taste.

The mountain crowberry's reddish creeping stems stand upright at their tips. Its many fine, leathery evergreen sessile leaves are 4–6 mm in length and curve inwards slightly, with a single whitish vein visible. It produces many inconspicuous (2–4 mm) pinkish or purplish-brown **flowers**, which are hermaphroditic (with both male and female reproductive organs). The three stamens, which extend far beyond the petals, are the flowers' most conspicuous feature. Its **fruit** takes the form of round berries (5–8 mm), which change from green to purple, and finally to a shiny black when ripe. The plants are generally abundant with fruit.

> ### DID YOU KNOW?
>
> **Common crowberry – *Empetrum nigrum* subsp. *nigrum***
> The plant's flowers are male or female rather than hermaphrodite and its branches are often capable of producing roots.
>
> ∿

↕	10–30 cm
✳	April/June
🍒	Mid-August/September
⛰	1200–2700 m
👄	Edible

Common crowberry, fruit.

Comon crowberry, male flowers.

Common crowberry, female flowers.

Bilberry, fruit (detail).

Bilberry, flower (detail).

BILBERRY

Vaccinium myrtillus · Ericaceae

Bilberry, fruit.

Found especially in upland areas and moorland such as Dartmoor and Exmoor, this plant is also known as whortleberry or European blueberry. While the berries are laborious to pick, they have traditionally been enjoyed in pies and tarts. However, their popularity seems to have been eclipsed by an American interloper – the blueberry. Though almost identical in appearance, blueberries, which are commercially grown, are larger in size; their flesh remains white inside and differs somewhat in taste.

The bilberry plant has many angular, upright, branched green stems. Its deciduous foliage consists of oval, light green alternate leaves with small petioles. The leaf edge is flattened and slightly dentate. Dark pink **flowers** grow from the leaf axils, individually or in pairs. The flower's calyx is made up of greenish sepals which adhere to the corolla. The petals form a small bell that hangs on a short peduncle. The surface of the **fruit**, bilberries, is covered with a bloom, giving them a frosted appearance. The berries are 5–8 mm in diameter and contain dark blue pulp from which juice can be extracted to make an effective dye. They have a particularly delightful flavour.

↕	30–50 cm
☀	April/June
⬥⬥	July/September
⛰	0–2600 m
👄	Edible

BILBERRY JAM

Harvesting the fruit

It is important to gather the fruit only when they are ripe and dry, never in wet weather.

The classic hand-picking method remains an excellent one, which yields clean fruit, though it can be rather time-consuming. Using a rake or comb picks up a number of unwanted extras, including dried or unripe fruit, leaves, and even small insects, which means that time must be spent sorting through the harvest. The picking season stretches from July to September in upland areas, depending on the altitude.

Ingredients

800 g granulated sugar for 1 kg fruit
1 lemon, preferably organic

Method

Wash the bilberries and allow to drain.

Place them in a pan with the granulated sugar and the finely grated zest of the lemon. Mix well. Gently boil the mixture for 30 minutes, stirring regularly with a wooden spoon.

Stir in the juice of the lemon 5 minutes before the end of cooking.

To test if the jam will set, place a plate in the refrigerator until it is cold. Pour a small amount of jam on the cold plate. If the mixture goes firm, it is ready.

Allow the jam to cool before pouring it into jars.

63

Bilberry, flowers.

Bog bilberry, flowers.

Vaccinium uliginosum subsp. *microphyllum*, fruit.

BOG BILBERRY

Vaccinium uliginosum · Ericaceae

Bog bilberry, fruit.

The bog bilberry and the bilberry (*Vaccinium myrtillus*) grow well with each other. Found in the same habitats, their branches can intermingle to such an extent as to cause confusion. However, if both species are picked while harvesting, there is no need for concern; when consumed in small quantities, bog bilberries will cause no harm.

The bog bilberry, also known as northern bilberry, favours acidic soils in subalpine ranges. Unlike the bilberry, its brownish stems are cylindrical. The oval, entire leaves are more than 1 cm wide, green and matt on top and greyish-green underneath, with clearly visible veins . It produces bell-shaped, white or pinkish **flowers** (4–5 mm) with peduncles much longer than its petals. The flowers form clusters of twos or threes at the leaf joints. The plant's **fruit** takes the form of round, blue berries (5–8 mm), which are covered with a dark bloom, giving them a frosted appearance. The juice from the berries is clear and has no particular taste.

‡	30–50 cm
✳	May/July
♦♦	August/Mid-October
▲▲	500–3000 m
☙	Unpalatable

DID YOU KNOW?

Vaccinium uliginosum subsp. *microphyllum*
The plant's leaves measure less than 1 cm and it has short peduncles (less than 3 mm).

〜

Bearberry, flowers.

Bearberry, leaves.

BEARBERRY

Arctostaphylos uva-ursi · Ericaceae

The plant's name implies that bears are fond of these singularly starchy berries. Bees and other insects are attracted to its flowers. The plant's leaves contain tannins, which were once used in the preparation of pelts. Today, its dried leaves, which have antiseptic and diuretic properties, are used in herbal medicine to treat minor urinary complaints.

Often confused with the bog bilberry, bearberry forms large colonies in dry grassy areas, pine forests, ravines, and sunny heaths. It grows at high altitudes in the south of England or colder climates such as Scandinavia and Scotland. The ends of its creeping stems stand erect. It has thick, dark green, entire evergreen leaves that are larger on the upper third of the plant. They have clearly visible veins on the more matt undersurface. It produces bell-shaped whitish or pinkish **flowers** (5–6 mm), which are clustered at the end of its stems. The plant's **fruit** takes the form of shiny red berries, which are 6–8 mm in diameter and stand out against its dark green foliage.

Bearberry, fruit.

Alpine bearberry, fruit.

DID YOU KNOW?

Alpine bearberry – *Arctostaphylos alpina*
The plant's finely dentate leaves have fine hairs along the edge and reticulate venation (smaller veins resembling a net) on both sides. Its fruit takes the form of a red berry that turns black when fully ripe.

↕	1–1.5 m
☀	March/July
♠	July/August
▲▲	500–2500 m
👄	Dried leaves

Osyris, flowers.

OSYRIS

Osyris alba · Santalaceae

Osyris, fruit.

Osyris grows in warmer parts of Europe such as Mediterranean but is absent from Britain. Like the mistletoe and field cow-wheat, it is a semi-parasitic plant. Through a system of projections known as haustoria, it parasitizes neighbouring plants to extract some of their sap while leaving enough to ensure their survival. Thus, the host and parasite are both able to grow normally.

This plant forms a small shrub with thin, angular, thornless stems which are slightly curved and sometimes creeping. Its small, hairless, lance-shaped leaves lack petioles. Large numbers of fragrant, yellowish male **flowers** form panicles to one side of the previous year's stems. The flower is made up of three lobes and three stamens. The single, yellowish, female flowers are found at the end of the stalks, on small terminal branches. The female flower's perianth is made up of three lobes and the style has three stigmas. Its inedible **fruit** are round fleshy drupes (4–8 mm), which go from green to bright red as they ripen and quickly take on a wrinkled appearance.

↕	0.6–1.2 m
✳	April/June
⚭	July/August
▲▲	0–500 m
✹	Unpalatable

Ma huang, fruit.

Sea grape, flowers.

Ephedra distachya · Ephedraceae

A long with horsetails and ferns, ephedra are some of the last remaining representatives of a distant era, the Carboniferous period, and can be regarded as a kind of living fossil. Their unusual shape attracts attention and the bright red fruit add a splash of colour to the landscape, particularly on sand dunes in dry areas of mainland Europe.

Highly branched, the sea grape can sometimes form large tufts. Its flexible, knotty, green branches are made up of segments of more than 3 cm in length. Tiny (2–3 mm) opposite leaves, joined at the base, form a sort of small sheath. It is a dioecious species, which means that its male and female reproductive organs are found on separate individuals. The discreet greenish **flowers** on its female stalks are surrounded by scales and stand upright in pairs on a small peduncle. The yellowish flowers of its male stalks form a catkin made up of 4–6 pairs of flowers. The plant's false **fruit**, which take the form of red berries, result from the swelling of the scales on the female plants. They become fleshy when ripe and form an aril (outgrowth) around the two seeds. The slightly sweet pulp of its fruit contains active alkaloids. Caution is advised.

Sea grape, fruit (detail).

Sea grape, fruit.

DID YOU KNOW?

Ma huang – *Ephedra major*
This plant's slender knotty branches stand upright. It has solitary female flowers. Its fruit is a false berry, which is red or orange in colour and contains a single seed.

↕	0.4–1 m
✳	May/June
♠	August/September
▲▲	0–1000 m
☠	Toxic

Subshrubs

Prickly pear, flowers.

PRICKLY PEAR

Opuntia ficus-indica · Cactaceae

Prickly pear, fruit.

Named after its prickly fruit, this plant can be found growing in old walls, on rocky slopes, in stony ground, on fallow land, or even beneath sunny hedges. It is also known as cactus pear and barbary fig, a name that derives from the fact that all foreign plants had the qualifier *barbare* ('roughly' or 'savagely' in Latin) in their names. The plant came from faraway Central America.

Prickly pear has flat spiny parts shaped like a tennis racket, known as cladophylls, that grow from its stem and take on a woody texture after a few years. It can grow to impressive heights. Its short-lived leaves are reduced to fine prickles that are found singly, in twos or in threes. Large, uniform yellowish or orange **flowers**, with many stamens and a widely spread corolla, form on the cladophylls. The skin of its fleshy, oval, yellowish or orange **fruit** is punctuated by prickles. The fruit's flesh is sweet and rich in vitamin C.

↕	2–3 m
✳	April/June
🍒	September/October
▲▲	0–300 m
👄	Edible

Gallic rose, stem and flowers.

Gallic rose, flowers.

GALLIC ROSE

Rosa gallica · Rosaceae

Thanks to the work of botanist and rose grower Charles Cochet-Cochet (1866–1936), we now know that the Gallic rose and the apothecary's rose are two distinct entities; he demonstrated that the famous apothecary's rose, or red rose of Lancaster, was a cross between the dog rose (*Rosa canina*) and the Gallic rose (*Rosa gallica*), which are both native to France. Highly regarded since 13th century, the Gallic rose has been used for its medicinal properties, in food preparation, and as a decorative flower.

Often found growing on sunny, dry hillsides, the Gallic rose has stems with large numbers of thorns of varying shapes and sizes. Its leaves are divided into five oval leaflets which are covered in hairs on the undersurface, where the veins are highly visible. Its bright purplish-pink, usually single **flowers** are relatively large (5–8 cm) and have a pleasant fragrance. They are attached to the stem via a long, glandular pedicel. Its accessory **fruit** takes the form of an oval, orange-red rose hip mottled with dark spots and covered in tiny glandular hairs.

Gallic rose, fruit.

↕	30–80 cm
☀	May/July
🌢	August/October
⛰	0–600 m
〰	Edible

Subshrubs

Dewberry, flowers.

DEWBERRY

Rubus caesius · Rosaceae

Dewberry, fruit.

The small, fragile dewberry often hybridizes with bramble plants to produce more robust offspring. Its fruit are rarely picked as they are only produced in small quantities and are located too close to the ground. The fact that they are covered in a powdery bloom, giving them a mouldy appearance, may also discourage picking. Dewberry is very often found in the company of its larger cousin, the bramble, which attracts the attention of foragers. Should the fruit of two species make their way into the same pot when jam is made, there is no need for concern as dewberry is edible.

The dewberry is found mainly in partially shaded habitats. Its branches, which are initially erect, then curved and tangled, are covered in small numbers of thin, short thorns. Its alternate leaves are made up of three dark green, unevenly dentate, hairy, lance-shaped leaflets, which are 15–25 mm in size. Only the terminal leaflet has a petiole. The leaves persist until winter. The **flowers** have white petals which sometimes have a pink tinge and are grouped in small clusters. They are 6–8 mm and clearly separated from each other, and the stamens and styles are about the same length. The **fruit** are made up of 3–12 tightly packed, blackish-blue drupelets, covered in a greyish waxy film and containing an acidic purple juice.

↕	30–70 cm
✳	May/June
🍒	August/October
⛰	0–1500 m
👄	Edible

Wild Fruit

Spurge olive, flowers.

Spurge olive, leaves and fruit.

SPURGE OLIVE

Cneorum tricoccon · Cneoraceae

Lizards play an active role in the propagation of this species. Found in the same rocky, sunny shrubland along the Mediterranean coastline, the reptiles are very fond of the spurge olive's fruit, and the seeds they expel establish new plants.

The plant's stems have numerous erect branches. Its alternate, oblong, leathery, relatively thick leaves are hairless and slightly curved at the edges. Each **flower** is made up of 3–4 bright yellow petals (6–10 mm in length), which are clearly separated, and an unobtrusive calyx made up of 3–4 green sepals. A single style with 3–4 stigmas is visible at the centre of the flower. The flowers grow from the axils of the plant's upper leaves, and are typically single or in pairs. Its **fruit** takes the form of a drupe, made up of 3–4 round chambers, each of which contains two seeds. The fruit have a smooth surface that becomes wrinkled as they age and change colour from green to red and then a brownish colour. The fruit of spurge olive may be confused with that of spindle *Euonymus europaeus*.

Spurge olive, fruit.

↕	60–90 cm
✳	April/June
🍒	August/September
▲▲	0–500 m
☠	Toxic

Corymb rose, fruit.

SHRUBS WITH RED FRUIT

These woody plants, which are multi-stemmed rather than having a central trunk, can reach 4 m or more in height. They may be deciduous or evergreen.

European barberry, flowers.

European barberry, fruit.

EUROPEAN BARBERRY

Berberis vulgaris · Berberidaceae

RECIPE

BARBERRY JELLY

Harvesting the fruit
The berries can be picked from mid-September, though some people wait until the first cold spell.

Ingredients
1 kg plain sugar or jam sugar
for 1 kg of juice

Method
Wash the fruit and remove any remaining stalks. Place them in a large saucepan and cover with water.
Cook the berries until they can be easily broken up with a wooden spoon. Filter the mixture through a sieve and squeeze the remaining fruit to extract as much liquid as possible. Add this to the sieved juice. Weigh the juice and add the required amount of sugar. Let the mixture sit for 2–3 hours. Cook the mixture in a saucepan until it forms a jelly. Pour it into sterilized jars and screw on the lids while it is still warm.

Unusually, this plant's wood is the same yellow as its flowers and its colour makes it popular for inlaid woodwork. The plant is also commonly used as a natural vegetable dye to produce yellow cotton, silk, wool, and even leather. In the past, there have been efforts to eradicate it from lowland areas, since a parasitic mushroom found on its leaves posed a threat to cereal crops. This threat has now been eliminated.

The plant prefers warm, chalky soil and full sun. Its spindly, ridged branches stand upright, then droop towards the ends. The many thorns are divided into three spikes. The oval, alternate leaves have a thick central vein and a short petiole. They are light green in spring and brownish in the summer. Large numbers of flower clusters, made up of 20–30 bright yellow **flowers**, are borne at the ends of the branches. The **fruit** take the form of elongated, purplish-red berries, about 1 cm in length, which form compact clusters. They have a slightly tart taste.

↕	1.5–3 m
✳	May/July
💧	September/November
▲▲	0–2000 m
👄	Edible

Flax-leaved daphne, inflorescence.

Flax-leaved daphne, flowers.

Daphne gnidium · Thymelaeaceae

In the past, this plant was used to treat ear complaints by placing small pieces of the stem inside the ear canal, a questionable practice given the plant's harmful effects. On contact with the skin, the toxic sap in its bark causes a reaction that leads to red blotches followed by unpleasant irritations.

Clustered together, the flax-leaved daphne's delicate reddish branches are easily broken. Its evergreen foliage is made up of elongated (2–5 cm), alternate, sessile leaves which taper to a point. The undersides of the leaves are paler than on top, where a central vein is clearly visible. Several yellowish-white **flowers** are clustered in panicles between the leaves at the ends of its branches; they have a hairy perianth surrounding eight stamens arranged in two rows. The flowering season is very long. The **fruit** take the forms of small (6–8 mm) orange-red berries which turn black as they ripen and are often visible among the plant's late flowers.

Flax-leaved daphne, fruit.

↕	0.6–2 m
✸	March/September
🫐	June/October
▲▲	0–800 m
☠	Toxic

Shrubs with Red Fruit

Mezereon, flowers.

Mezereon, inflorescences.

Mezereon, fruit.

MEZEREON

Daphne mezereum · Thymelaeaceae

White mezereon, flowers.

White mezereon, fruit.

This is a very attractive plant at a time of year when flowers are in short supply; as winter draws to a close, lovely little pink flowers appear before its leaves open. However, it is highly toxic.

The plant's upright stems are covered in grey bark and its branches are hairy. The **flowers** have a lilac-rose-coloured perianth, which is covered with silky hairs and composed of petals and sepals which are indistinguishable. They are borne in small clusters on the stems and have a pleasant fragrance. Its lance-shaped, alternate leaves, which are 5–10 cm long and form a sort of tuft, are found at the end of its stems. The plant's shiny bright red **fruit** takes the form of berries, 6–10 mm in diameter and containing a single seed.

↕	40–100 cm
✳	February/Mid-April
⚬⚬	June/September
▲▲	300–2500 m
☠	Toxic

DID YOU KNOW?

White mezereon –
Daphne mezereum var. *alba*
The plant is identical in appearance except for
its white flowers and yellow fruit.

∿

Wild Fruit

Tutsan, flowers.

TUTSAN

Hypericum androsaemum · Hypericaceae

The plant's common name tutsan is a corruption of the French *toute saine*, which literally means 'all-healthy', a nod to its alleged healing and medicinal properties. It is also known by the common name of St John's Wort. Nowadays, the plant is no longer used for medical purposes but is a favourite of florists, who use both the flowers and berries in floral arrangements. It is common in the wild in Britain.

The tutsan's somewhat woody branches are marked with two clearly visible symmetrical lines. Its rather large (6–10 cm) green leaves, which lack a petiole, are sometimes heart-shaped and are lighter on the underside. The small golden-yellow **flowers**, which have large numbers of stamens, are most often found at the end of its branches. Its **fruit** takes the form of oval berries, which turn from green, to red then black and contain many tiny seeds. The sepals are clearly visible at the base of the berries, as are the remains of three styles at the end.

Tutsan, fruit.

↕	40–100 cm
☀	Mid-June/August
🍒	August/September
⛰	0–1500 m
🌿	Unpalatable

Shrubs with Red Fruit

Alpine honeysuckle, flowers.

A variety whose fruit are only partially fused.

ALPINE HONEYSUCKLE

Lonicera alpigena · Caprifoliaceae

Alpine honeysuckle, fruit.

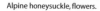

DID YOU KNOW?

Lonicera alpigena var. *semiconnata*
The two parts of this variety's fruit are only partially fused.

〜〜

↕	1–2 m
☀	May/July
🍒	August/September
▲▲	600–2000 m
☒	Toxic

This honeysuckle has particularly attractive red fruit, which are uniformly distributed among the leaves. Their cherry-like appearance is deceptive, as they are in fact poisonous. Caution is advised, especially with young children, who can easily reach them. The plant has a squat appearance and, like the honeyberry and black honeysuckle, it is found mainly in upland areas. It is also commonly used as a hedging plant.

The alpine honeysuckle favours damp, shady areas of beech and fir woods. Its trunk, which has brown bark, supports young downy branches scattered with raised pores known as lenticels. Its opposite leaves, which are much longer than wide, end in a narrow point. Veins are clearly visible on the shiny underside of its leaves. The reddish, sometimes yellowish **flowers** are 15–20 mm in diameter and are supported by long peduncles that emerge from the base of the leaves. The flower's corolla consists of a large lower lip and an upper lip formed from the fusing of four other petals. The long stamens are topped with red anthers. They are in fact double flowers whose fused ovaries have become one. The **fruit** takes the form of shiny, oval, bright red berries with two small black dots on the surface which are scars from its ovaries. The berries are twin fruit that have been fused together.

Etruscan honeysuckle, flowers.

Etruscan honeysuckle, leaves and flower buds.

ETRUSCAN HONEYSUCKLE

Lonicera etrusca · Caprifoliaceae

truria was an ancient region of Italy which roughly corresponds to modern-day Tuscany. The region's mild climate produced a number of remarkable species of plants, among them the Etruscan honeysuckle, which has beautiful, symmetrical flowers with a lovely fragrance.

The species' preferred habitats are light woods, forest edges, hedges, and undergrowth. Its hairy branches produce slightly hairy, deciduous foliage. The lower leaves have only very short petioles, while the upper leaves are attached directly to the stem. The plant's yellowish and pinkish **flowers** form terminal clusters of three flowerheads on top of a long pedicel which grows from an elongated peduncle. The stamens are much longer than the tube that forms the corolla, which ends in a four-lobed upper lip and a lower lip. The flower's calyx is in the shape of a ring with five points. The plant's **fruit** takes the form of oval red berries, clustered at the ends of its branches.

Etruscan honeysuckle, fruit.

↕	2–3 m
☀	May/July
🍒	August/Mid-October
▲▲	0–1500 m
❀	Toxic

Shrubs with Red Fruit

Pyrenean honeysuckle, flowers.

Pyrenean honeysuckle, leaves and fruit.

PYRENEAN HONEYSUCKLE

Lonicera pyrenaica · Caprifoliaceae

Pyrenean honeysuckle, fruit.

This plant is found only at high altitudes, colonizing grassy patches and rocky outcrops and favouring relatively damp, silty, alkaline soil. It is far less common than the alpine honeysuckle and is primarily found in the Pyrenees, from where it gets its name.

The plant's generally upright branches have greyish bark, which comes off in long strips. Its deciduous oblong leaves are hairless and narrow towards the petiole; they remain relatively small at 2–4 cm. Pairs of pinkish-white **flowers**, with peduncles roughly the same length as the flowers, appear at the leaf joint. The flower's corolla is made up of five lobes. Two distinct ovaries are joined at the base of the flowers, which are extremely fragrant and attract large numbers of insects that ensure its pollination. Its **fruit** takes the form of round, orange-red berries which form slightly fused pairs.

↕	0.8–1.5 m
☀	Mid-May/July
🍒	August–September
▲▲	800–1500 m
☠	Toxic

Fly honeysuckle, inflorescences.

Fly honeysuckle, flowers.

FLY HONEYSUCKLE

Lonicera xylosteum · Caprifoliaceae

The flexible hollow branches of fly honeysuckle are used to manufacture brooms. Its wood can also be used to smoke meat or fish and the fruit are a favourite of certain species of birds, including warblers and thrushes.

The fly honeysuckle's stems are initially upright, then drooping at their ends. The wood of its mature branches is hollow and its grey bark splits into thin strips. Its hairy, opposite, entire leaves, are longer (3–5 cm) than they are wide (1–1.5 cm). Its branches bear many flower clusters, made up of two pairs of **flowers**, which are attached to the stem via a peduncle. Slightly fragrant and yellowish-white, they consist of a two-lipped corolla 10–15mm long, with five stamens of the same length. The plant's **fruit** takes the form of fragrant bright red berries, fused in pairs, which are often confused with red-currants. They look enticing, but the utmost caution is advised, as just a few berries are enough to poison a child.

Fly honeysuckle, leaves and fruit.

Fly honeysuckle, fruit.

↕	1–2 m
☀	May/Mid-June
🍒	July/August
▲▲	100–1600 m
☠	Toxic

Chinese boxthorn, fruit.

Boxthorn, flower.

BOXTHORN

Lycium barbarum · Solanaceae

Boxthorn, fruit.

This plant grows in virtually any type of soil and is found in all manner of habitats, sometimes on sites where no other plant would take root. However, it is always found in warm spots that get plenty of sun.

The plant's tufted appearance results from its many long, pliable branches, which have very few thorns. Its thin, narrow, greyish leaves, entire and lance-shaped, are 3–6 cm long. Small, tightly clustered or single **flowers** are attached to long pedicels (2–3 cm) that emerge from just above where the leaf meets the stem. The flower's calyx consists of five irregular teeth, while its lilac-purple corolla is made up of a tube terminating in five lobes from which the stamens emerge. The plant's **fruit**, known as goji berries, are shiny, soft-fleshed, elongated, orange-red berries, which are roughly 1–1.5 cm in length. The remains of the flower's calyx are clearly visible at the base of the berries. Care should be taken when harvesting as the berries have a passing resemblance to woody nightshade.

↕	1–1.5 m
✳	July/September
⬦⬦	August/October
⏶⏶	0–700 m
✖	Raw: slightly toxic
👄	Dried: edible in small quantities

DID YOU KNOW?

Chinese boxthorn – *Lycium chinense*
The flower's calyx is made up of five identical teeth. The species has become naturalized in some parts of Europe.

～

Mastic tree, female flowers.

Mastic tree, male flowers.

MASTIC TREE

Pistacia lentiscus · Anacardiaceae

The wood of this plant exudes a fragrant, clear resin that congeals when it comes into contact with air. Known as mastic, it is traditionally produced on the Greek island of Chios in the Aegean Sea, where the tree has been cultivated for centuries. It grows only in warm Mediterranean climates. The resin is used in various ways, including in food, cosmetics, and paint.

Favouring heat and full sun, the mastic tree is a dioecious species, with male and female reproductive organs on separate plants. It forms an evergreen bush with greyish-brown bark, which is smooth at first and becomes rough. It has small (2–4 cm) alternate leaves that are divided into even numbers of 4–12 leaflets. The leaves are supported by winged petioles. Spikes of small, densely packed flowers that measure only a few millimetres appear at the leaf joints. The inconspicuous female **flowers** are covered in matted woolly down, and turn from red to black. The male flowers remain the same deep red colour as the flower's stamens. The plant produces small **fruit** in the form of an inedible drupe, which is not quite round and ends in short, sharp point. The drupes retain their red colour for quite some time before turning black. The fruit are borne in clusters, each containing a single seed.

Mastic tree, fruit.

↕	1.5–5 m
✺	April/July
🍂	October/November
⛰	0–900 m
👄	Fruit: inedible. Resin: edible

Shrubs with Red Fruit

Terebinth, male flowers.

Terebinth, female flowers.

Pistacia × saportae, fruit.

TEREBINTH

Pistacia terebinthus · Anacardiaceae

Terebinth, fruit.

DID YOU KNOW?

Pistacia × saportae **is a hybrid of** *P. lentiscus* **and** *P. terebinthus*.
Its leaves, which remain on the plant for an extended period of time, are made up of an uneven number of leaflets and its fruit form small clusters.

~~

↕	2–5 m
✳	April/June
🍒	September/October
▲▲	0–700 m
👄	Edible

Sharing the same habitats as the mastic tree (see p.83), the terebinth tolerates shade, and can be found along the forest edge. Its uses are equally varied. Its fruit, pickled in vinegar, can be served as a condiment. Terebinth essential oil is extracted from the resin produced by the plant. In autumn, its leaves take on bright colours to create a flamboyant display. Reddish scabs caused by aphids appear on some of the plant's leaves and were once used to dye certain types of cloth.

A slow-growing plant, the terebinth gives off a characteristically resinous odour. The smooth, brownish bark becomes rough with age. Its leaves are divided into an uneven number of leaflets, ranging from seven to eleven. The oblong, lance-shaped, leathery leaflets are shiny on top. Unlike the mastic tree, the petioles are not winged. Dense clusters of **flowers** form just above the leaf joints of the previous year's branches. It is a dieoceous species, the female flowers remaining green and featuring a style with three stigmas, while the male flowers are more colourful, with red stamens. The plant's **fruit** are aromatic drupes, which have a slightly tart flavour. Their surface is punctuated with tiny white spots, and they turn from red to a bluish colour when ripe. A pair of small points are visible at the end of the berries.

Alpine currant, flowers.

ALPINE CURRANT

Ribes alpinum · Grossulariaceae

Despite its name, the alpine currant is found in a wide range of habitats across Britain (mainly the north) and mainland Europe. Originally described from alpine specimens, its name still reflects this, although the plant will grow in lowland areas, woodlands and hedges. It makes a pleasing addition to the landscape, with its attractive flowers and yellowish foliage in autumn.

The plant's upright stems are covered in a greyish bark which is gradually shed as they age. Its leaves, which are shiny on top, are divided into three or five dentate lobes in the shape of a polygon. This is the only member of the genus *Ribes* which is dioecious, with male and female reproductive organs on separate plants. Its greenish **flowers**, with petals that are broad at the ends and tapered at the base, form small, erect clusters. The 10–20 male flowers are more numerous than the female flowers, which number only 3–5. The lance-shaped bracts are just as long, or longer than, the flowers' peduncles. The plant produces **fruit** in the form of translucent berries, which change from a yellowish colour to orange and then red as they age.

Alpine currant, fruit.

↕	0.8–1.5 m
✳	April/May
◔◔	July/August
▲▲	300–1800 m
👄	Edible but bland

Shrubs with Red Fruit

Rock redcurrant, flowers.

ROCK REDCURRANT

Ribes petraeum · Grossulariaceae

Rock redcurrant, fruit.

As its name suggests, the plant grows readily amid rocks and stones, where it is often found. The genus *Ribes* is native to northeastern Europe but grows as a garden plant elsewhere. It spread from the shores of the Baltic Sea to Flanders and south to the Pyrenees. The plant needs the cold of the winter months to ensure the rise of its sap in spring, but cannot tolerate late frosts.

The plant's dense, tight branches have a greyish bark that comes away in small sections. Its strongly dentate, hairy leaves can reach 8–12 cm in length and have long petioles. The leaves are divided into 3–5 creased lobes. Its reddish **flowers** form clusters that initially spread outwards and then droop. The sepals are broad at the end and tapered at the base, while its petals are wedge-shaped. Its **fruit** takes the form of smooth, bright red berries, arranged in hanging clusters. They have a slightly tart taste.

↕	0.5–1.5 m
✳	May/June
🍒	August/September
▲▲	500–2100 m
👄	Moderately edible

Redcurrant, flowers.

REDCURRANT

Ribes rubrum · Grossulariaceae

This plant's growth gets underway very quickly as spring rolls in; before the trees spread their leaves, it takes advantage of the light that reaches the undergrowth. Its new shoots are easy to spot from far away, which makes it a good time to locate specimens to be picked later in the season. However, the plant's small range does somewhat limit the potential fruit yield, as do the birds which like to feed on them. Fortunately, there are occasionally some remaining berries.

The upright branches are covered in a greyish bark that blackens as it ages. The slightly hairy leaves, with petioles the same length as the blades (4–8 cm), are divided into heart-shaped lobes. The profusely borne creamy yellow **flowers**, which have long sepals and much shorter petals, resemble a coup sundae glass in shape and form loose, hanging clusters. The **fruit** takes the form of translucent, shiny, hairless, bright red berries, 8–10 mm in diameter and possessing a slightly tart flavour. The plant is easy to grow, with many cultivars developed from the wild species for use in gardens and orchards.

Redcurrant, fruit.

↕	1–1.5 m
✴	Late March/Early May
🍒	July/August
⛰	0–2000 m
👄	Edible

Raspberry, fruit.

Raspberry, flower and unripe fruit.

RASPBERRY

Rubus idaeus · Rosaceae

Raspberry, fruit (detail).

Raspberries are a lot less vigorous than their close cousin the blackberry, and as a result they are found in much smaller numbers in the wild. They will grow as far north as the Arctic Circle and are often found in clearings, along roadsides, in rocky areas with full sun, and on light soil. There are many recipes for transforming the fruit into jams and jellies, either on their own or paired with other wild fruit, such as bilberries or blackberries.

The raspberry's branches are biennial, and thus the new, upright stems will not bear flowers or fruit in the first year. The stems have sparse small, reddish thorns and the alternate leaves are composed of 5–7 oval dentate leaflets, light green on top and covered with white woolly hairs underneath. Its **flowers** form panicles at the ends of its two-year-old branches and have a whitish corolla (8–10 mm) with spaced, curved petals which surround numerous stamens. Its dull red **fruit**, the raspberry, is made up of a collection of drupelets with distinct furrows between them, and is easily detached from the plant when ripe.

↕	0.5–1.5 m
✴	May/August
🍒	July/September
▲▲	100–2000 m
👄	Edible

Cotoneaster juranus, flowers.

Common cotoneaster, flowers.

COMMON COTONEASTER

Cotoneaster integerrimus · Rosaceae

This cotoneaster is most often found in mountainous areas, on steep rocky slopes with full sun, but also in undergrowth. A pioneer species, it adapts quickly, even in harsh environments. The genus *Cotoneaster* is constantly evolving, with new species arising from genetic modification to colonize very specific micro-habitats.

The plant's brownish bark is hairy at the ends of its young branches but becomes hairless on older plants. Its oval, 2–3 cm, entire leaves are covered in a layer of matted woolly hairs on the underside and have a petiole which is hairless or only very slightly hairy. The inconspicuous pinkish **flowers** (5–7 mm) emerge in twos or threes from just above the leaf joint, the five short petals barely extending past the calyx. The plant produces a roundish accessory **fruit** (6–8 mm), which is hairless and turns from orange to red as it ripens. It has a floury texture and contains 2–4 seeds.

Common cotoneaster, fruit.

DID YOU KNOW?

Cotoneaster juranus
The undersides of the leaves of this earlier-fruiting species are very hairy.

Cotoneaster delphinensis
This plant features slender branches and its flowers are supported by long peduncles.

〜

↕	0.5–1.5 m
✳	May/June
🍒	July/September
▲▲	500–1500 m
✺	Unpalatable

Shrubs with Red Fruit

Hairy cotoneaster, flowers.

HAIRY COTONEASTER

Cotoneaster tomentosus · Rosaceae

Hairy cotoneaster, fruit.

The Nebrodi mountain range in Sicily has lent its name to a number of plant species. Among these are two species of fleshy fruit, *Ephedra nebrodensis* and the hairy cotoneaster, which goes by the scientific name *Cotoneaster nebrodensis*. It is found in chalky soil and favours rocky or stony slopes with good sun exposure.

Its very hairy young branches bear fairly long (4–6 cm) alternate leaves which are nearly round. Both sides of the young leaves are covered in a layer of matted woolly down. Its **flowers** hang from their hairy peduncles in clusters of 3–6. The flower's corolla barely extends farther than the hairy calyx, with sepals that are reddish on the outside and greyish-pink inside. The plant produces red, semi-round **fruit** of 5–8 mm in length, covered in cottony white hairs. They contain 3–5 hard seeds.

↕	1–1.5 m
☀	April/June
🍒	August/October
▲▲	600–1800 m
✹	Unpalatable

Wild Fruit

Field rose, flowers.

FIELD ROSE

Rosa arvensis · Rosaceae

The species name means 'in the fields', which implies that this plant is restricted to open countryside. However, it is also found in shaded habitats, such as forest fringes, shrub thickets, and along woodland trails, and at higher altitudes, on the lower slopes of mountains. It has a trailing habit, producing stems that are borne close to the ground. Slender stipules surround the base of the petiole. Its large, white, single **flowers**, which are supported on long, hairy pedicels (15–25 mm), have fused styles that form a column topped by a flat disc.

The field rose's long, flexible stems retain their green colour and have sparse small, slightly curved thorns. Its deciduous, alternate leaves are made of up 5–7 relatively small oval leaflets with a roughly dentate blade. The flower's pointed mature sepals curve slightly and are eventually shed by the plant. Its accessory **fruit** takes the form of a rounded, smooth, dull red, elongated rosehip (1–1.5 cm) with a small round scar at its end.

Field rose, fruit.

↕	0.5–1 m
✳	May/July
⚭	August/September
▲▲	0–1400 m
👄	Edible, once seeds are removed

Dog rose, flowers.

DOG ROSE

Rosa canina · Rosaceae

Dog rose, fruit.

O ne of the most common wild roses, this plant was once used to treat bites from rabid dogs, hence its name *Rosa canina*, or dog rose. The remedy goes back to ancient times, with no mention of its origins to be found in medical texts. The plant's fruit, which contain a layer of hairs around the seeds, can be used in all manner of culinary concoctions, including jams, fruit pastes and syrups, wines, soups and even as a flavouring in beer!

The plant's many long branches, which are erect or spreading, are equipped with hooked thorns. Its deciduous, alternate leaves are divided into five or seven dentate leaflets. The long petiole can be hairless or slightly hairy. At the base of the petioles are elongated stipules, which taper to a point. The pink or white **flowers** (4–5 cm), which have no fragrance, are found individually or in clusters of four or five. The flowers shed their sepals when they reach maturity. The accessory **fruit** is a smooth, bright red, oval-shaped rose hip that results from the swelling of the floral receptacle and can grow to up to 2 cm in length. Tucked away inside the fruit are very hard seeds and hairs that can cause irritation. The fruit contains some of the highest concentrations of vitamin C of any wild fruit species.

↕	2–4 m
☀	May/July
♠♠	August/October
▲▲	0–1500 m
⬯	Edible, once seeds are removed

ROSE HIP JELLY

Harvesting the fruit
Wait until after the first frosts to pick the rose hips. It is strongly
recommended that you wear gloves to do so, as this is a very thorny shrub.

Ingredients
Equal parts of sugar and juice from the hips. Jam sugar can also be used.
Juice of 1 lemon

Method
Set aside plenty of time.
Wash the rose hips. Remove the peduncle from one end and the black cap
from the other.
Cut the hips in two, deseed it, and remove the hairs.
Place the hips in a saucepan, cover with water, and cook for an hour on
medium heat, until they have softened.
Keep an eye on the water level and add more if needed.
Strain the mixture and set the juice aside.
Pass the rest of the mixture through a fine-sieved food mill to extract
the flesh.
Press the mixture in a sieve to extract any remaining juice.
Add this liquid to the strained juice along with an equal weight of sugar
and the lemon juice. Bring to a boil, and occasionally skim any froth that
forms at the surface.
To check whether the jelly will set, place a plate in the refrigerator. When it
is cold, pour a few drops of the jelly on it. If it firms up, it is ready.
Pour the jelly into jars and cover once they have cooled.

ROSE HIP WINE

Ingredients
1 kg rose hips
800 g sugar

Method
Pick the fruit after they have been softened by the first frosts – remember to wear
gloves.
Remove the peduncles and the black bits at the top.
To make the syrup, put the sugar in a saucepan containing 800 g water and mix
well.
Heat the mixture to boiling point and boil for 30 seconds. Allow to cool.

Place the fruit in a glass bottle and pour the syrup over it. Cover the bottle opening
with muslin.
Allow to macerate for two months, while stirring the mixture regularly.
Strain the liquid and pour into bottles that seal well. Allow the wine to stand for
two to three months before consuming.
The wine can be served cold as an apéritif or paired with melon and cured ham.

Persian yellow rose, flowers.

PERSIAN YELLOW ROSE

Rosa foetida · Rosaceae

Persian yellow rose, fruit.

Originally indigenous to Asia, this plant became naturalized in Austria and France. It went largely unnoticed for many years and it was thanks to Joseph Pernet-Ducher, a rose grower from Lyon in France, that it rose to prominence at the end of the 19th century. After several years of painstaking research, his experiments led to the development of a yellow garden rose which was met with immediate success on account of its bright colour.

The Persian yellow rose has slender stems dotted with thorns, which are denser at the base and more sparse at the top. Its alternate, clearly dentate leaves are made up of 5–7 oval leaflets, which are lighter-coloured underneath. The leaves are attached to the branches by a short petiole. The plant's single **flowers** have large petals, stamens, and a pistil which are all bright yellow. They have an unpleasant odour, to which the rose owes its scientific name, derived from the Latin *fetere*, 'to stink'. The accessory **fruit** is a round, smooth rose hip (1–1.5 cm) that turns from green to a brownish red as it ripens. The withered remains of the flower's calyx are visible at the top of the fruit.

↕	1.5–2 m
☀	May/June
🍒	August/September
⛰	200–1100 m
🚫	Unpalatable

Red-leaved rose, flowers.

RED-LEAVED ROSE

Rosa glauca · Rosaceae

This mountain rose's beauty lies in the contrast between its red stems and its bluish-green, purple-tinged leaves. It is often planted as an ornamental shrub in gardens, squares, and city parks. In autumn, its colourful fruit, which remain on the plant for an extended period and are of little interest to birds, provide an additional attraction.

The plant's rather thick stems have a slight bloom and are covered in a small number of curved thorns. Its leaves are made up of 5–9, fairly long (2–3 cm), lance-shaped leaflets, which have dentate edges around two-thirds of their perimeters, usually tapering out around the petiole. The plant produces clusters of 3–5 scentless **flowers**. They have a fuchsia-pink corolla made up of large petals and a calyx that consists of long sepals, three of which are entire, and two divided. The flowers are short-lived. The accessory **fruit** is a round, hairless, brownish rose hip, which bears the remains of the flower's calyx until it is eventually shed.

Red-leaved rose, fruit.

↕	1–2 m
☀	June/August
🍒	September/October
▲▲	800–2000 m
👄	Edible, once seeds are removed

Shrubs with Red Fruit

Cinnamon rose, flower.

Cinnamon rose, thorns.

CINNAMON ROSE

Rosa majalis · Rosaceae

Cinnamon rose, fruit.

Like the lily of the valley, the cinnamon rose flowers in May – hence the shared name *majalis*. This early-flowering species caught gardeners' attention as early as the 16th century, and was subsequently used in developing new garden varieties. The cinnamon rose is part of the section *Cinnamonae*, along with *Rosa pendulina* and *R. rugosa*. It is also known by the scientific name *R. cinnamomea*. Its preferred habitats are rocky slopes, scrub and sloping banks.

Forming large bushes, the plant's interwoven stems have slightly curved thorns, which are found in pairs at the nodes. Its oval leaves are hairy beneath and divided into five or seven roughly dentate leaflets. Its **flowers** are borne along the stems and are composed of lilac-pink petals (3–5 cm) and entire sepals that are the same length as the petals. They are followed by an accessory fruit or false fruit in the form of a rather small, round rose hip, which turns from green to orange and then bright red. The **fruit** has a smooth, shiny surface and the remains of the flower's calyx stand erect at the top.

↕	1.5–2.5 m
✳	April/May
⚭	July/August
⛰	300–2000 m
👄	Edible, once seeds are removed

Corymb rose, fruit.

Alpine rose, flowers.

ALPINE ROSE

Rosa pendulina · Rosaceae

For a relaxing break from a walk, one only needs to stop to observe the alpine rose's fruit, the shape of a spinning top with a colourful, shiny surface. The plant can be found under the shelter of beech trees or on rocky banks in mainland Europe.

Straight thorns are distributed along its slender stems, sparsely towards the top and more densely at the base. Its oval deciduous leaves are made up of 7–9 long leaflets, which are darker on the underside. The edge of the leaf blade is doubly dentate and large stipules adorn the base of its petioles. The **flowers** are distributed evenly over the plant, individually or in groups of two or three. They are carried on long peduncles (3–4 cm) covered in many small glandular hairs. The flower's sepals can sometimes be seen extending beyond its large (1–1.5 cm), rounded, purplish-pink petals. Its accessory **fruit** takes the form of red rose hips, shaped like a spinning top or pear, with the remains of the flower's calyx at the top. The smooth surface is occasionally covered with small glandular hairs.

Alpine rose, fruit.

↕	1–1.5 m
✳	May/July
⚭	August/September
▲▲	500–2400 m
👄	Edible, once seeds are removed

Shrubs with Red Fruit

Small-flowered sweet briar, thorns.

Small-leaved sweet briar, flower.

SWEET BRIAR

Rosa rubiginosa · Rosaceae

Sweet briar, fruit.

Sweet briar, flowers.

L ess widespread than the dog rose but present all over Britain and Europe, this plant bears a strong resemblance to the classic species but it is less vigorous. Another distinguishing feature can be detected by rubbing its leaf between the fingers, when it releases a subtle aroma of green apples.

The plant's thick, upright stems have variably sized hook-shaped thorns which are thicker at the base. Its alternate leaves are divided into many rounded, dentate leaflets. The stipule at the base of the petiole is covered in small glandular hairs. This rose produces clusters of pink **flowers**, which have a pleasant fragrance, and pinnate leaves. The flowers' rather short (1–1.5 cm) peduncles are covered in fine, straight, glandular hairs. The **fruit** takes the form of rose hips, which change from orange-red to red and bear the remains of the flower's calyx on the top. They are rather small and have a few glandular hairs on their surface.

↕	2–3 m
✳	June/July
◊◊	August/October
▲▲	0–1,600 m
〰	Edible, once seeds are removed

DID YOU KNOW?

Small-leaved sweet briar – *Rosa agrestis*
The plant's thick thorns are hooked at the ends. Its white flowers have a pinkish tinge and its ripe fruit are hairless.

Small-flowered sweet briar – *Rosa micrantha*
The plant's thorns are curved and the remains of the flower's calyx can be found at the top of its fruit.

〜〜

Japanese rose, variety with white flowers.

Japanese rose, flower.

JAPANESE ROSE

Rosa rugosa · Rosaceae

Found in a wide range of natural habitats, the Japanese rose is commonly used as an ornamental plant in decorative gardens. It is native to Asia and is very robust. It is also exceptionally resistant to disease and it can even grow in salty coastal habitats, including those in Britain. The plant's roots produce suckers that allow it to spread, so much so that it is considered an invasive species in Scandinavia. The plant's hardiness is its main weapon in displacing local indigenous species.

The plant's leafy, hairy, upright stems form dense bushes. They have numerous curved, bristly thorns of varying size. The thick, rough-textured leaves have prominent veins and are covered in fine, short hairs. The leaves are divided into 5–9 oval leaflets. The plant produces **flowers** made up of a calyx of five sepals and a corolla of long crimson petals. Its **fruit** takes the form of thick, shiny, red rose hips, which are slightly flattened at both ends.

Japanese rose, fruit.

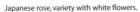

DID YOU KNOW?

Rosa rugosa var. *alba*
This rose has white crinkled petals.

∾

↕	0.5–1.5 m
✳	May/July
🍒	August/October
▲▲	0–700 m
👄	Edible, once seeds are removed

Shrubs with Red Fruit

Evergreen rose, flowers.

EVERGREEN ROSE

Rosa sempervirens · Rosaceae

Evergreen rose, fruit.

The evergreen rose hybridizes readily with other species. It is often found crossed with the field rose, which can produce fertile specimens with modified forms, such as sharply dentate or larger leaves and lush inflorescences. It prefers heat and full sun, and can be found along forest fringes, beside hedges, and on dunes and scrubland.

The plant forms a sprawling bush made up of long climbing stems with sparse curved thorns. Narrow stipules are present around each petiole. Its evergreen leaves are divided into five shiny, leathery, finely dentate leaflets which taper to a point. The plant's rather large (4–6 cm) white **flowers**, which are made up of five notched petals and five oval pointed sepals, cluster to form small corymbs. It produces accessory **fruit** in the form of a small (1 cm), oval, hairy rose hip, which turns from green to red and has a short point at the end.

↕	3–6 m
✴	May/June
🍒	July/September
⛰	0–700 m
✂	Unpalatable

Apple rose, green fruit.

Harsh downy-rose, flowers.

HARSH DOWNY-ROSE

Rosa tomentosa · Rosaceae

There is a group of roses known as 'downy roses', of which the harsh downy-rose is a prime example. These roses have glandular hairs on their leaves, sepals and fruit. The harsh downy-rose gets its name from its leaves, which have a layer of matted hairs.

The plant favours dry, sunny spots, including the forest edge, rocky ground, and hedges. Its many stems have mostly straight, reddish thorns. Its downy, oval leaves are made up of 5–7 bluish-green dentate leaflets. Its fairly large, light pink, single **flowers** are distributed evenly among its stems. The calyx is made up of two entire sepals, two symmetrically lobed sepals, and one partly lobed, partly entire sepal. The relatively long pedicels (1.5–2 cm) are covered in straight glandular hairs. Its accessory **fruit** takes the form of oval or round, orange to bright red rose hips, topped with what remains of the flower's calyx. Their surface is densely covered with hairs.

Harsh downy-rose, fruit.

↕	1–2 m
✳	June/July
🝆	September/October
▲▲	0–1400 m
👄	Edible, once seeds are removed

Shrubs with Red Fruit

Blackberry, fruit.

SHRUBS WITH NON-RED FRUIT

These woody plants can reach a height of 4 metres or more. They are multi-stemmed, with no discernible trunk, and may be deciduous or evergreen.

Wild asparagus, leaves.

Wild asparagus, young shoots.

WILD ASPARAGUS

Asparagus acutifolius · Asparagaceae

Wild asparagus, green fruit.

The sandy scrubland of the Mediterranean coast is the only area in which this plant grows, and come February it is buzzing with activity as foragers hunt for young wild asparagus shoots. Their task is made much easier by the young plant's soft green colour, which contrasts sharply against the darker adult plants. In spite of their slightly bitter taste, the spears are delicious in omelettes and other dishes and are highly sought after.

This bushy, woody plant is made up of many rough, curved, greenish branches. Their fairly short (3–6 mm) cladophylls (flattened leaf-like projections), are grouped in clusters of 5–12, and are slightly prickly to the touch. The plant's yellowish **flowers**, which are found singly or in pairs, are supported by short, articulated peduncles. The flowers are dioecious, with male and female reproductive organs on separate plants. The male flowers have six stamens, while the female flowers have a small, projecting style. The **fruit** takes the form of a pea-sized berry that turns from green to black and contains three seeds. The berries are toxic.

↕	0.6–1.3 m
✳	June/Mid-August
🍒	August/September
▲▲	0–800 m
〜	Spears: Edible
🦐	Berries: Toxic

Common yellow jasmine, fruit.

Common yellow jasmine, flowers.

COMMON YELLOW JASMINE

Jasminum fruticans · Oleaceae

The aromatic compounds produced by the various species of jasmine combine to make a much-loved fragrance. In Asia, jasmine is traditionally associated with femininity. Mock orange flowers are often mistaken for jasmine, but in fact they belong to a completely different genus, *Philadelphus*.

Also known as wild jasmine, the common yellow jasmine plant stands erect. Its woody stems divide into fragile, angular, green branches. It has shiny, oblong, alternate leaves, which are semi-evergreen, shedding their leaves in cold winters but keeping them in mild ones. The leaves are either simple and entire, or divided into three lobes. Before they appear, fragrant yellow **flowers** in clusters of 2–4 form at the top of the branches. The flower's calyx, made up of rounded sepals, is much smaller than the corolla. One or two stamens can be found inside the corolla. The plant's **fruit** takes the form of black berries, 4–8 mm in diameter, which are shiny at maturity. The species favours sunny, dry, rocky slopes and limestone rock crevices such as those found in southern Europe.

Winter jasmine, flowers.

DID YOU KNOW?

Winter jasmine – *Jasminum nudiflorum* flowers in winter.
Its yellow corolla is tube-shaped and it is often grown as a decorative plant.

〜〜

↕	0.5–1.5 m
✹	May/September
🌢	August/October
▲▲	0–1000 m
☠	Toxic

Honeyberry, flowers.

HONEYBERRY

Lonicera caerulea · Caprifoliaceae

Honeyberry, fruit.

Also known as blue honeysuckle, this plant has berries that are easily mistaken for bilberries, as they are nearly identical in colour and shape. To tell them apart, one must look at their stems, which are angular on the bilberry and rounded on the honeyberry, or compare the size – the honeyberry is distinctly larger.

The honeyberry's brownish or reddish bark comes off in small strips. It has deciduous, oval, pointed leaves, which are slightly darker on top and slightly hairy when young. Tiny petioles attach the leaves to the branches. The plant produces yellowish-white **flowers** in the shape of small, elongated, slanted bells, which are supported by short peduncles. The flowers are always found in pairs whose ovaries are completely fused. Its **fruit** takes the form of an elongated blue berry which results from the fusing of the two ovaries, which form a small blister at the end of the berry. The berries are covered in a powdery bloom. This is quite a rare species, which prefers damp woods, thickets, marshes and scrub.

↕	0.7–1 m
✳	April/Mid-July
🍒	July/Mid-September
⛰	1200–2300 m
🥄	Edible

DID YOU KNOW?

Lonicera caerulea var. *edulus*, native to Siberia, China and Japan, produces delicious edible berries that are similar to blueberries. It can be grown in Britain and Europe as a garden plant.

〜〜

Black-berried honeysuckle, flowers.

BLACK-BERRIED HONEYSUCKLE

Lonicera nigra · Caprifoliaceae

Preferring acid soil, this honeysuckle is found on high ground, among fir trees, and in damp shaded forests and thickets. Sites where it is found to be growing should not be disturbed, as the plant is extremely rare. In addition to fir trees, it is found among rowan trees, bilberries, holly, and raspberries. It shares these habitats with the black woodpecker and the rare boreal owl.

The plant's brownish stems produce quite large, deciduous, oval leaves, which taper to a point. The leaves have short petioles. The foliage sometimes darkens early, giving the bushes a lovely hue of red ochre. The **flowers** are produced in pairs, supported by a long pedicel, and seem to rest on the leaves. The white corolla (8–10 mm) has a pinkish tinge and a neat lower lip. Its ovaries are barely fused at their base and its stamens extend far beyond the corolla. Its **fruit** takes the form of bluish-black berries, found in pairs at the end of a shared peduncle. Their purplish flesh contains 4–8 unevenly shaped seeds.

Black-berried honeysuckle, fruit.

DID YOU KNOW?

Leycesteria formosa, Himalayan honeysuckle (also called pheasant berry) is a garden escapee that grows in wild areas close to habitation. Once the calyces have turned brown, the berries taste like toffee.

↕	1–2 m
✳	April/July
🍂	July/Early September
⛰	500–1700 m
☠	Toxic

Shrubs with Non-red Fruit

Boxleaf honeysuckle, flowers.

Shrubby honeysuckle, fruit.

BOXLEAF HONEYSUCKLE

Lonicera nitida · Caprifoliaceae

Boxleaf honeysuckle, fruit.

Introduced to Europe barely a century ago, this Chinese species continues to spread, growing well in a number of habitats. The plant makes an excellent ground cover, which is why it can be found in many parks, public gardens, and roadsides. Among its unique characteristics are its purple fruit, which are impossible to miss, in spite of the fact that some of them remain hidden beneath its leaves. The plant is susceptible to extended periods of frost in winter. It is often mistaken for box because of its small leaves.

This is a slightly creeping plant, with a bushy appearance. It has opposite, oval, evergreen leaves, which have a shiny, leathery texture. Its pairs of discreet pale yellow **flowers** are particularly fragrant and attract bees and other insects. Flowering begins on the outer branches and progresses inwards. Its **fruit** are shiny, round, purple-violet berries, which are fused in pairs at the base and appear to be glued to the stems.

↕	1–1.5 m
✳	May/June
◌	September/October
▲▲	0–500 m
☠	Toxic

Blackcurrant, flowers.

BLACKCURRANT

Ribes nigrum · Grossulariaceae

The only species of wild currant that produces black fruit, this plant grows in semi-shade and is common in hedgerows throughout Europe. Commercial cultivation of the fruit has increased in recent years to meet growing demand. The plant's fruit and leaves are rich in anthocyanins and have long been used as a cardiovascular tonic. An early-flowering species, its buds are used in the preparation of some homeopathic remedies.

The plant's young bark is yellowish-brown and tends to darken with age. Its alternate leaves are made of three or five triangular, roughly dentate lobes. On the underside of the leaves, a number of greenish glands give off a pleasant aroma, particularly when rubbed. Its discreet, bell-shaped, red and green **flowers** form small hanging clusters. The flower is made up of five hairy, curved sepals, which are longer than the petals that surround the five stamens and single style. The plant's **fruit**, the blackcurrant, takes the form of a shiny black berry with small grey glandular spots, borne in small hanging clusters. The small greyish bit at the end of the berry is what remains of the flower's calyx.

Blackcurrant, fruit.

↕	1.5–1.8 m
☀	Mid-April/May
🍒	July/August
⛰	300–1500 m
👄	Edible

Shrubs with Non-red Fruit

Gooseberry, flowers.

GOOSEBERRY

Ribes uva-crispa · Grossulariaceae

Gooseberry, fruit.

The plant is known as *groseille à maquereau* or mackerel berry in French, as it is traditionally served as an accompaniment to mackerel. However, the English name gooseberry does not necessarily indicate the berry is served with goose (although it can be!). The berries can be eaten raw, cooked in pies and tarts or preserved as jam. A fairly common and widespread species, it prefers nitrate-rich soil.

The plant forms bushes with greyish-black bark. Its many branches are studded with thorns made up of three fine, straight points. Its slightly hairy, alternate leaves are divided into three or five semi-circular serrated lobes. Discreet **flowers**, found singly or in pairs, are evenly distributed on the plant. They are composed of reddish or greenish sepals, which are curved or spread out, and thinner, whitish petals. The flower is attached to the stem via a small peduncle. Its **fruit** are round, translucent, yellowish berries that measure 1–2 cm in diameter and are largely covered with small straight hairs. The berries' thick skins encase a slightly tart-tasting flesh.

↕	1–1.5 m
✳	March/April
🍒	June/August
▲▲	100–1600 m
☠	Toxic

Snowberry, specimen with lobed leaves.

Snowberry, flowers.

SNOWBERRY

Symphoricarpos albus · Caprifoliaceae

The white fruit of this remarkable species have inspired all manner of fanciful comparisons. Depending on the season, the berries can resemble pearls or small snowballs, hence the name. Children love to play with them. In some languages the white berries are referred to as corpseberries or ghostberries, as it is said they provide nourishment for wandering spirits.

The lower parts of this bushy plant's branches stand upright, while the upper parts are curved. The plant's oval, opposite, entire leaves are dark green on top and blue-green underneath. Its bell-shaped, white or pink **flowers** are arranged in dense clusters of 3–8 flowers that form just above where the terminal leaves meet the branches. The flower's corolla is made up of five lobed petals, which are very hairy inside. Its **fruit** are spherical, white berries, which are 5–15 mm in diameter and often have spots. They contain a soft pulp and two or three seeds and are toxic.

Snowberry, fruit.

↕	1–2 m
☀	May/September
⬥⬥	September/November
⛰	0–1200 m
☠	Toxic

Shrubs with Non-red Fruit

Spurge laurel, fruit.

Spurge laurel, flowers.

SPURGE LAUREL

Daphne laureola · Thymelaeaceae

Dwarf spurge laurel, leafy stems.

As winter comes to a close, spurge laurel is one of the first plants to flower. Its fruit differs from that of other daphnes in that they are elongated rather than round and blackish as opposed to red or orange. The hardness of the stems is another distinguishing factor.

This evergreen species favours soils that are rich in humus. Its leathery, rather long (3–10 cm), alternate leaves are shiny on top and darker underneath. The leaves are only found on the ends of its stems and are larger towards the top. Short clusters of **flowers** appear at the base of the leaves; they are small (8–10 mm), yellowish-green and have short pedicels. The plant's rather abundant oval **fruit** are 7–9 mm in diameter and change from green to purplish-black as they age. The berries can remain on the plant until the beginning of winter.

↕	0.5–1 m
☀	January/April
🜕	June/August
⛰	0–1600 m
☠	Toxic

DID YOU KNOW?

Dwarf spurge laurel –
Daphne laureola* subsp. *philippei
Covered in leaves nearly from the ground up, the plant's many stems stay close to the ground, with only the tips of the branches standing upright. The stems range from 30 to 50 cm in length.

～∾

Wild privet, flowers.

WILD PRIVET

Ligustrum vulgare · Oleaceae

The plant's botanical name comes from the Latin *ligare*, which means 'to knot' or 'to fasten'. Like willow, its young branches can be used in wickerwork. This characteristic flexibility and strength can also be found in its more mature wood, which was once used to produce lances and later skis and the sticks used in certain forms of martial art.

The plant is fond of sun, but can also tolerate the shade of the forest edge and light woodland. Its foliage persists for some time into winter. Its upright, opposite branches are covered in greyish bark and are very flexible. Narrow, pointed, opposite leaves are attached to the branch by a small petiole and the small, fragrant, whitish **flowers** are arranged in panicles. Some quickly become dry and turn brown. The flower's calyx has four lobes and its tubular corolla has four lobes at its opening. The plant produces **fruit** in the form of shiny black berries, which are 6–7 mm in diameter and contain 2–4 seeds. The berries form dense clusters, which remain on the plant for the better part of winter.

Wild privet, fruit.

↕	1.5–3 m
✳	May/July
🍒	September/November
⛰	0–1100 m
☠	Toxic

Narrow-leaved mock privet, flowers.

NARROW-LEAVED MOCK PRIVET

Phillyrea angustifolia · Oleaceae

Narrow-leaved mock privet, fruit.

This plant is often mistaken for an olive tree, which has similar elongated, evergreen leaves, but the two plants differ in their fruit. Another plant with which it is sometimes confused is the Italian buckthorn, though the two species can be distinguished by looking at the arrangement of their leaves. The plant sometimes forms small colonies on abandoned fields and is also found along roadsides, on scrubland, and dry, sunny forest fringe.

It is an evergreen bush with spindly, upright branches, which are covered in light grey bark. As its name points out, its leathery leaves are quite narrow, measuring 6–10 mm in width and 5–7 cm in length. The lance-shaped, opposite leaves have an entire leaf blade, which is shiny on top and on which a maximum of six pairs of side veins are visible. Each leaf is supported by a tiny petiole. Small, fragrant, yellowish or greenish **flowers** form round clusters at its leaf joints. The flowers have two stamens and their calyx and corolla are both made up of four parts. The plant's **fruit** takes the form of a drupe, which changes from purplish-red to black, and is covered in a grey bloom. The drupes have a small, distinct point at the end and contain a stone with two seeds.

↕	1.5–3 m
☀	March/June
⚭	September/October
⛰	0–900 m
✗	Unpalatable

Prunus × fruticans, fruit.

Blackthorn, flowers.

BLACKTHORN

Prunus spinosa · Rosaceae

The blackthorn's fruit remain attached to the plant for a prolonged period, long after its leaves have fallen. They can remain on the branches long enough to face the first frosts, which will soften the acidity of their flesh (as will home-freezing). This is the ideal time to pick the fruit to make jams, liqueurs or sloe gin. The berries are generally not eaten raw, on account of their astringent taste. However, the seeds were found in the stomach contents of Neolithic man and it is possible to become accustomed to the taste. The plant is sometimes crossed with plum trees.

Blackthorn, which readily produces suckers, forms dense, thick bushes. Its very thorny branches have blackish-grey bark and bear small oblong deciduous leaves in an alternate arrangement. The leaves' finely dentate blade is hairy and then becomes smooth, except on the veins on the underside of the leaf, which remain hairy. Hundreds of small **flowers** appear on all of its branches at the start of spring. Found singly or in pairs, they are spread evenly along the branches, lending them an ethereal quality. The flowers are attached to the stem via a brownish-green peduncle. The **fruit**, called sloe, take the form of blackish-blue drupes covered in a light powdery bloom, giving the young fruit a matt appearance. The fruit's oval stone is slightly rough.

Blackthorn, fruit.

> **DID YOU KNOW?**
>
> *Prunus × fruticans*
> Thorns are few or non-existent on the plant's branches. Its fruit are larger.
>
> ᔕᔕ

↕	1–4 m
✳	March/April
🍒	August/October
⛰	0–800 m
👄	Edible

Italian buckthorn, flowers.

ITALIAN BUCKTHORN

Rhamnus alaternus · Rhamnaceae

Italian buckthorn, fruit.

↕	2–4 m	
✳	March/April	
🍒	October/November	
⛰	0–1000 m	
☠	Toxic	

A golden-yellow substance can be extracted from the bark and unripe fruit of this plant. It was at one time widely used as a dye to brighten silks and other fabrics and was also used by painters – by mixing it with white clay or alum, they obtained a product that gave excellent results. In the early days of painting, achieving different hues of green proved rather difficult. To do so, colouring compounds derived from plants of the Rhamnaceae family were used, including the alder buckthorn, buckthorn, and Italian buckthorn. This elusive green hue became a symbol in its own right in religious art.

A thornless, evergreen bush, the plant is dioecious, with male and female reproductive organs on separate plants. Its greyish or dark brown bark wrinkles as it ages. Its leathery, alternate leaves, which come in different shapes, are shiny on top. The leaf edges are always dentate and surrounded by a hard but flexible, cartilage-like substance. Tiny yellowish, male or female **flowers** cluster together to form the inflorescences. The five lance-shaped sepals are erect on the female flowers and folded back on the male flowers. The flowers lack a corolla and have five stamens that surround a style that is divided into two or three parts by a deep cleft. The **fruit** takes the form of drupes, supported by short peduncles, that change from a reddish colour to black as they ripen. They do not generally exceed 6 mm in diameter.

Rhamnus saxatilis subsp. *infectoria*, flowers.

Avignon berry, flowers.

AVIGNON BERRY

Rhamnus saxatilis · Rhamnaceae

Avignon berry looks like small blackthorn, since both are very thorny and scraggly and have similar leaves. They can be easily told apart by their fruit, however, which are blue on the blackthorn and black on the Avignon berry. A sun-loving species, it prefers lower mountain slopes with their poor soil, rocky heaths, woods and scrub. It is also found on chalky plateaus. In Britain, it is generally found only in cultivation.

The plant has highly branched, slanting stems with long thorns at their tips. It is a dioecious species, with male and female reproductive organs on separate plants. Its 2–3 cm, lance-shaped, slightly dentate leaves become narrower towards the petiole, the length of which is around one-fifth that of the leaf blade. The yellowish **flowers** form small clusters. The calyx is made up of four lance-shaped lobes, while the corolla, with its four pointed petals, forms a cross. The **fruit** takes the form of fairly small (4–6 mm) round drupes, which turn from red to black and are known as Avignon berries. They are effectively dispersed by birds.

Avignon berry, fruit.

DID YOU KNOW?

Rhamnus saxatilis subsp. *infectoria*
The plant's petioles are about a third of the size of its leaf blades. The flowers are hermaphroditic, containing both male and female reproductive organs. It is not found above 700 m in altitude.

↕	0.6–1 m
☀	April/May
🍒	August/September
⛰	0–1300 m
☠	Toxic

Shrubs with Non-red Fruit

Laurustinus, flowers.

LAURUSTINUS

Viburnum tinus · Caprifoliaceae

Laurustinus, fruit.

The plant's common name could refer to the fact that its leaves resemble those of the cherry laurel – but the resemblance ends there, as the metallic blue colour of its fruit and very long flowering time set it apart from the latter. Experiments with plants from the genus *Viburnum* have resulted in many interesting cultivars. The species *Viburnum davidii*, with its dark blue set against fruit bright green foliage, is particularly attractive and makes a lovely addition to the garden.

The plant's thick, squarish, slightly downy branches have a brownish bark with many raised pores. Its leathery, oval, simple, nearly pointed leaves are in an opposite arrangement. They are very shiny on top and measure 4–8 cm in length. The **flowers**, which develop from pinkish buds to mature white flowers, form small corymbs. They consist of a calyx composed of five sepals that taper to a point, a corolla of five rounded lobes, five stamens with yellow anthers, and a single style. The **fruit** takes the form of an elongated drupe, whose metallic blue colour eventually turns black.

↕	2–3 m
✹	October/June
♠	August/September
▲▲	0–700 m
◡	Edible

Briançon apricot, flowers.

Prunus brigantina · Rosaceae

The seeds of the Briançon apricot were once ground to extract a vegetable oil known in France as *huile des marmottes*, or marmot oil. Indeed, its nut-like seeds are rich in edible fats that can be used as a substitute for olive oil in many dishes. The oil was also formerly used in lamps. The plant is a wild relative of the almond and native to France and Italy, where it mainly grows.

The Briançon apricot's sprawling branches are covered in a greyish, slightly cracked bark. Its fairly large (5–7 cm), oval leaves, which are darker on top, are supported by small reddish petioles. The leaf blade, with irregular sharp teeth along its edges, has clearly visible hairy veins running through it. The plant's white **flowers**, which appear before its leaves, are attached by very tiny peduncles and form small clusters of 3–5. The corolla has rounded, 6–8 mm long petals. The **fruit**, which resemble little yellow plums, are produced in small bunches and seem glued to the branches. They are shiny, 2–3 cm drupes with yellowish flesh, which have an unpleasant taste.

Briançon apricot, fruit.

↕	4–6 m
✴	April/May
🍂	Mid-August/September
⛰	800–1700 m
🦫	Unpalatable

Redoul, flowers.

REDOUL

Coriaria myrtifolia · Coriariaceae

Redoul, fruit.

Rich in tannins, this plant was long used to tan leather and indeed its botanical name derives from the Latin *corium*, which means 'leather'. The black colouring extracted from its fruit was also used as a dye. Its common name of redoul comes from Occitan, the medieval language of Languedoc, and refers to the intoxicated state observed in goats when they eat its young shoots, of which they are rather fond. The goats begin to tremble and dance bizarrely and often ultimately die from the poison. Redoul grows mainly in the Mediterranean and is not found in Britain.

The plant prefers a sunny location and chalky soil. Its angular stem bears many flexible, curved, opposite branches, and its oval leaves end in a small point and resemble myrtle leaves. Three veins are clearly visible on its light green, undulate leaf blades, which are attached via a shortened petiole that spreads somewhat on the branch. Small, greenish **flowers** form sprawling clusters. The calyx has five sepals that intertwine with the five petals that make up the corolla, which contains ten stamens and very thin reddish styles. Redoul produces shiny, black accessory **fruit**. When fruiting begins, the floral organs become fleshy and turn a blood red colour. They progressively curve to surround the fruit and turn black. When ripe, the fruit resemble blackberries, for which they are all too often mistaken – dangerously so, as the plant is extremely toxic.

↕	1.5–3 m
☀	April/July
♠	August/September
▲▲	0–700 m
☠	Toxic

Burnet rose, flowers.

Burnet rose, thorns and fruit.

BURNET ROSE

Rosa pimpinellifolia · Rosaceae

Of all the rose species, the burnet rose is the only one to bear black fruit. Another distinguishing feature is that its stems are covered in vast numbers of thorns. In autumn, its small leaves take on a lovely coppery hue. This unusual rose is quite rare, even though it is found over a wide geographical range. It requires plenty of sun but will grow in acid or chalky soil. In upland areas, its branches stand straight and upright, while in coastal areas it takes on a more twisted appearance and its fruit appear more reddish.

The plant's straight or curving stems readily produce suckers. The stems are covered in large numbers of straight thorns, which vary in length. The deciduous, alternate leaves are composed of 5–11 small dentate, oval, hairless leaflets that are lighter on top. The **flowers** are profusely borne and have a white or pink-tinged corolla and a calyx that consists of stiff, lance-shaped sepals. Its accessory **fruit** are round, purplish or black rose hips with a smooth, shiny surface. The hardened remains of the flower's calyx can be seen on the ripe fruit. The peduncle (2–3 cm) is much longer than the fruit itself and is sometimes covered in stiff hairs.

Burnet rose, fruit.

↕	0.3–1 m
✳	May/July
🍒	September/October
▲▲	0–1800 m
👄	Edible

Shrubs with Non-red Fruit

Blackberry, flowers.

Rubus canescens, leaves.

Blackberry, fruit.

BLACKBERRY

Rubus fruticosus · Rosaceae

= BLACKBERRY & = ELDERBERRY WINE

Ingredients
1 kg black elderberries
1 kg blackberries
1.5 kg caster sugar
3 litres water
20 g baker's yeast

Method
Wash the fruit. In a saucepan, dissolve the sugar in the water and add the fruit. Bring to a boil and boil for 20–25 minutes. Decant the liquid into a demijohn while simultaneously adding the yeast. Allow to stand for 10 days, stirring the mixture daily. Filter the mixture, return it to the demijohn and allow to ferment for 40 days. Carefully decant the wine into bottles. The wine should be consumed fairly quickly, as it does not keep well.

Several hundred distinct microspecies fall under the umbrella of *Rubus fruticosus*. Though the berries seem superficially similar from one microspecies to the next, on closer inspection differences begin to emerge in their first year's stems, thorns, young branches, flowers, and fruit. They all form tangled bramble bushes, which are quick to colonize open spaces. The botanical name derives from the Latin *frutex*, which means bush or shrub.

The blackberry's stems stand upright the first year, and then begin to curve and form layers the following year. They are covered in thorns, which can be either hooked or straight. The deciduous, occasionally persistent leaves are divided into three or five dentate, pointed, hairless leaflets. The plant produces whitish or pinkish **flowers** with a corolla of spaced petals. Its compound **fruit**, the blackberry, is made up of small, very shiny drupelets which turn from red to black when ripe.

↕	1–2 m
☀	May/August
◌◌	July/October
⛰	0–1500 m
👄	Edible

DID YOU KNOW?

Rubus canescens
The plant's leaves are covered in a layer of matted woolly down, which gives it a whitish appearance.

∼∽

Savin juniper, flowers.

SAVIN JUNIPER

Juniperus sabina · Cupressaceae

This mountain species is found at high altitudes among boulders and on dry grassy patches. Rubbing its branches vigorously releases a rather unpleasant odour that results from the presence of particularly toxic compounds. Using the branches to produce essential oils or other preparations is unsafe.

The plant's twisted branches form a thick, wide-spreading bush. Its bark is a light brownish-grey. The plant's older leaves are reduced to diamond-shaped scales, applied in many rows, one after the other. The lance-shaped, prickly, scale-like leaves on its younger branches are less tightly packed. It bears rather inconspicuous, cone-like **flowers**, with male and female flowers on the same plant. The plant's tiny round **fruit** is in fact a false berry, or modified cone, known as a galbulus, that becomes fleshy and berry-like as it matures. The galbulus, which is blackish-blue and covered in a powdery bloom, contains a few seeds and is attached to the branch via a short peduncle. All of the plant's fruit ripen during the same year, which means that unripe fruit from the previous year are not found alongside ripe fruit, as is the case with some junipers.

Savin juniper, fruit

↕	1.5–2 m
✳	April/May
🍒	September
⛰	1500–2500 m
☠	Toxic

Shrubs with Non-red Fruit

Red bryony, fruit.

CLIMBING PLANTS

The pliable stems of these plants can grow very long and require supports for the plant to develop fully. Some species are herbaceous (for example bryony and black bryony), while others, such as wild grape and common honeysuckle, are woody.

Red bryony, female flowers.

Red bryony, male flowers.

RED BRYONY

Bryonia dioica · Cucurbitaceae

Red bryony, fruit.

This creeper grows at a spectacular rate, in just a few weeks, it can reach a height of 4–5 m and cover part or all of its support. In autumn, its many fruit, clustered in multi-coloured garlands that snake through the greenery, draw the admiration of passers-by. However, as attractive as they may be to look at, the plant is toxic. It is often confused with black bryony, another climbing species.

The red bryony's male and female plants are distinct. They grow from an impressive root, in the shape of a turnip, and attach to their supports by means of long, spiralling tendrils. The hairy leaves are divided into five lobes and wither quickly, giving the plant an autumnal appearance. The **flowers** are about 1 cm in size, the larger, yellowish male flowers supported by a long peduncle, while the female flowers are greenish in colour. The plant's abundant **fruit** takes the form of round berries, which turn from green to yellow, to orange, and finally to red as they age.

↕	3–5 m
✳	May/June
🍒	September/October
⛰	0–1600 m
☠	Toxic

Bridal creeper, flowers.

Elide asparagoides · Asparagaceae

Native to South Africa, this plant was inadvertently introduced to Europe and has become naturalized in coastal areas of the Mediterranean. It has spread so quickly there that it is classed as an invasive alien species, and is being monitored to evaluate the risks it poses and, where possible, to limit its spread and impact on other plant species.

Coastal dunes and cliffs are the plant's preferred habitats, but it also colonizes shrubby areas. Its leathery, entire leaves form an alternate arrangement along its creeping stem. The shiny, heart-shaped leaves are quite wide at the base and taper to a point at the end. Veins are clearly visible on the leaves. A number of white **flowers**, found singly or in pairs, appear at the leaf joints. The flower's calyx is made up of five small triangular sepals and its petals, which have a pale green central fissure running along their length, are folded in the middle, exposing a cluster of stamens with orange anthers. Its **fruit** takes the form of small red berries that eventually turn black.

Bridal creeper, fruit.

↕	1–3 m
☀	March/April
🍒	Mid-August/September
▲▲	0–100 m
☠	Toxic

Perfoliate honeysuckle, flowers.

ITALIAN HONEYSUCKLE

Lonicera caprifolium · Caprifoliaceae

Perfoliate honeysuckle, fruit.

Unlike the Etruscan honeysuckle (see p.79), Italian honeysuckle is a climbing species. The plant prefers a more temperate climate and is found along hedgerows and forest fringes, occasionally in Britain. Commonly grown as a garden plant, it often succeeds in escaping from gardens to colonize surrounding areas. The plant is also frequently hybridized with other species of honeysuckle to create new cultivars.

This honeysuckle winds its way around its support. Its downy young stems have leathery, deciduous leaves with a thin translucent margin. The fragrant, pink and yellowish **flowers** tend to fuse to form a flat plate. The downy tube of the flower's corolla is quite long. The **fruit** takes the form of bright red oval berries that form tight clusters at the ends of their peduncles.

↕	2–4 m
✳	Mid-April/Mid-June
🍒	Mid-July/September
▲▲	0–1200 m
☠	Toxic

Minorca honeysuckle, leaves and fruit.

Minorca honeysuckle, flowers.

Lonicera implexa · Caprifoliaceae

When a plant finds a favourable habitat, it tends to establish itself permanently. A section of preserved forest near Tarascon in southern France is one such habitat, which is home to an important and diverse collection of Mediterranean flora. The Minorca honeysuckle can be found here, amid holm oaks, wild madder, pistachio trees and sarsaparillas.

The plant's leathery, evergreen, oblong leaves are opposite. Slightly bluer on the undersurface, they have pinkish margins. The terminal leaves are fused and surround the stalk. Lightly fragrant **flowers**, which lack a peduncle and change colour from pink to yellow to white, appear at the leaf joints. The tube-shaped corolla is divided into two lips: an upper lip, which results from the coming together of four rounded lobes, and a lower lip formed by the fifth lobe. The **fruit** takes the form of round berries, which are found in clusters of four or five inside the terminal leaves, which form a sort of bowl. The mature berries are orange-red in colour.

Minorca honeysuckle, fruit.

↕	0.5–2 m
☀	May/July
♠	Mid-August/Mid-October
▲▲	0–700 m
☣	Toxic

Common honeysuckle, flowers.

Common honeysuckle, variety with lobed leaves.

COMMON HONEYSUCKLE

Lonicera periclymenum · Caprifoliaceae

Common honeysuckle, fruit.

The flowers of the common honeysuckle release a subtle, heady, evanescent fragrance and as night approaches, their sweet aroma pervades the air. The fragrance is intended to attract butterflies and moths in order to ensure the species' pollination and reproduction.

The plant's many intertwined stems form diffuse bushes with the plants that support it. Its oval, entire, opposite leaves have tiny petioles at the base of the stems and become sessile at the tips of the branches. They may be downy or smooth. Fragrant reddish **flowers**, which turn white or yellowish, appear at the ends of the stems. The elongated corolla (4–5 cm) consists of a tube that opens into two lips: a large upper lip with four points and a drooping, entire lower lip. Prominent stamens with yellow anthers emerge from the flower. Its **fruit** takes the form of shiny, oval, red berries found in small clusters at the leaf joints and on the ends of the branches. Their surface has a slightly sticky appearance.

↕	5–7 m
☀	June/August
🌢	September/October
▲▲	0–1100 m
☠	Toxic

DID YOU KNOW?

Lonicera periclymenum var. *quercinum*
This variety has wavy lobed leaves like those on an oak tree.

〜〜

Sarsaparilla, flower buds.

Sarsaparilla, mature flowers.

Smilax aspera · Smilacaceae

The long clusters of colourful fruit produced by sarsaparilla brighten up overgrown hedges. In France and southern Europe where the plant grows, its berries can easily be confused with red bryony berries. However, the latter's leaves will have withered or dropped by the time its fruit reach maturity. Another species for which it is frequently mistaken is the black bryony, which has similar leaves, but again they are deciduous, which leaves the sarsaparilla identifiable by its evergreen foliage.

The plant's slightly spiny stems harden with maturity and become rough and angular. They coil around supports by means of pairs of small tendrils located at the base of the leaves. Its dark green, heart- or arrow-shaped, alternate leaves are shiny on top and develop spines along their edges. The petioles and main vein are also spiny. Its whitish, sessile **flowers** consist of a small perianth with six yellowish points, and six stamens or three stigmas. The flowers are dioecious (male and female reproductive organs on separate plants) and form small, fragrant clusters. Its **fruit** takes the form of shiny, rather small berries (7–8 mm) that turn from green to yellow then red. The berries are divided into three sections and contain 1–3 round seeds.

Sarsaparilla, fruit.

↕	2–3 m
☀	August/November
🍒	February/May (of the following year)
▲▲	0–400 m
☠	Toxic

Climbing Plants

Black bryony, female flowers.

Black bryony, male flowers.

BLACK BRYONY

Tamus communis · Dioscoreaceae

Black bryony, fruit.

Long ago, the black bryony was among a panoply of remedies used to treat the after-effects of blows to the body; the roots were cooked and applied as a paste to swollen areas. Paradoxically, the same roots, uncooked, cause small blisters when they come into contact with the skin. Indeed, they were even used by some as means of giving the appearance of having sustained abuse in an attempt to seek charity from others.

The plant is a dioecious species (with male and female flowers on separate plants), which prefers sunny spots with moist soil. From its substantial rhizome grow striated stems, which either twine with neighbouring plants that provide support or follow the dried remains of the previous year's stems. Its heart- and lance-shaped, alternate leaves have branched palmate veins (radiating from one point). The plant's inconspicuous **flowers** (4–6 mm) have a yellowish-green perianth. Its male flowers are arranged in a loose spike, while its female flowers are clustered in small, compact racemes. Its **fruit** takes the form of strings of berries, which turn from green to yellow then red when ripe. They remain on the plant among the dried leaves for a long time.

↕	2–4 m
✳	April/September
🍒	August/October
▲▲	0–1300 m
🐟	Fruit: Toxic
👄	Young shoots: Edible

Wild Fruit

Berry-bearing catchfly, flowers.

Berry-bearing catchfly, flowers.

Cucubalus baccifer · Caryophyllaceae

The fine, star-shaped flowers of this plant are reminiscent of Greater stitchwort, *Stellaria holostea*, while its shiny fruit resemble those of deadly nightshade (see p.49), for which they can easily be mistaken. These striking features must have inspired the artists responsible for creating the six medieval *Lady and the Unicorn* tapestries. The plant's flower and fruit appear on one of them, a feat made all the more impressive by the fact that this inconspicuous plant is rather elusive in its natural environment. It is only when it bears its fruit that it becomes easier to spot.

The plant's thin stems, which are easily broken, grow from a creeping rootstock. The stems are covered in rough hairs that allow them to cling on to neighbouring species for support. Its oval leaves end in small points and are attached to the stems by short petioles. Its hanging, greenish and pinkish white, bell-shaped **flowers** have a bulbous calyx that ends in five uneven lobes. The corolla consists of petals divided in two by a deep cleft, with about ten stamens surrounding three styles. Its **fruit** takes the form of shiny, round, black berries, which are 5–8 mm in diameter and have the thread-like remains of the flower at the end. The plant is found along hedges and streams, and in scrub habitats and damp forests.

Berry-bearing catchfly, fruit.

↕	0.5–1.5 m
☀	July/September
🍂	September/October
▲▲	0–600 m
🐛	Unpalatable

Climbing Plants

Common ivy, flowers.

COMMON IVY

Hedera helix · Araliaceae

Common ivy, fruit.

Flowering late in autumn, the common ivy provides an important source of nourishment for a number of insect species, including bees, which are particularly fond of its pollen. Its fruit appear in the middle of the winter, providing a new source of sustenance for birds such as thrushes, blackbirds and other passerine species, and persist until spring.

Common ivy either sprawls or climb by short, root-like stems. Its leathery, alternate leaves are shiny and dark green. Depending on their position on the plant's stems, the leaves take on different shapes: entire on the stems bearing the inflorescences and with 3–5 lobes on the other branches. Its many hermaphrodite **flowers** form umbels. The flower's corolla is made up of five yellow petals. Its **fruit** takes the form of round, bluish-black berries with five ridges, which are 7–9 mm thick and have a small bump on top. The berries are toxic, but their hardness and bitter flavour mean that they are almost always immediately spat out when tasted.

↕	20–25 m
☀	September/November
🍒	January/April (of the following year)
▲▲	0–1100 m
🦋	Toxic

Boston ivy, fruit.

Boston ivy, flowers.

Parthenocissus tricuspidata · Vitaceae

During the summer, this verdant species seems rather uninteresting, a form of green cover among many others. At best, it is useful cover for a crumbling wall or a sad-looking façade. In autumn, things begin to change and its leaves take on remarkable hues that range from coppery-orange to reddish-brown that inject a flamboyant splash of colour to shrubs and hedgerows.

A fast-growing species, the plant climbs by means of tendrils, which end in small cup-like pads that adhere to surfaces. Its thick, shiny leaves are divided into three pointed lobes and attached to the reddish branches by short, squat petioles. Its yellowish-green **flowers** form barely visible loose clusters under its leaves. The plant's **fruit** takes the form of bluish berries, arranged in open clusters. They have a rather bland flavour and are unpalatable, except to birds. Commonly grown as an ornamental, the species has become naturalized in partly shaded and sunny habitats in Europe. Also known as Japanese ivy, the plant gets its common names from its resemblance to ivy.

Virginia creeper, fruit.

DID YOU KNOW?

Virginia creeper –
Parthenocissus quinquefolia
The plant's leaves have palmate veins (several primary veins radiating from a point) and are divided into five lobes.

∿

↕	10–15 m
✳	May/June
🌢	September/October
▲▲	0–500 m
✖	Unpalatable

Climbing Plants

Wild madder, flowers.

Wild madder, fruit.

WILD MADDER

Rubia peregrina · Rubiaceae

Madder, flowers.

The plant's botanical name provides some clues to the ways in which it can be used. *Rubia* is Latin for 'red', which refers to the scarlet and crimson colouring obtained from the plant and particularly its roots. These natural hues were long used as dyes, and gave bright colour to military uniforms in the days before camouflage. The word *peregrina* derives from the same Latin root as 'peregrinate' – to wander about from place to place – a rather apt description this plant's propensity to colonize the right habitat.

The square, climbing or creeping stems of wild madder are covered in prickles which curve downwards. Its sessile, oval and lance-shaped, evergreen leaves are arranged in whorls. They are glossy, with toothed margins. Small **flowers** appear at the leaf joints as well as at the ends of the stems. The flower has no calyx and its corolla is made of five yellowish petals that form a tube. Its **fruit** takes the form of round black berries, 4–6 mm in diameter.

↕	2–4 m
✳	June/July
🍒	August/September
▲▲	0–1200 m
✖	Inedible

DID YOU KNOW?

Madder – *Rubia tinctorum*
A collection of smaller veins forming a network are visible on the underside of the leaf.
The flower's petals are yellow. Its fruit takes the form of a berry, roughly the size of a pea, which changes from purplish to black and has a slight depression on the end. A red colouring, known as madder, is extracted from its roots.

Wild grape, leaves and fruit.

Wild grape, fruit.

WILD GRAPE

Vitis vinifera subsp. *sylvestris* · Vitaceae

This very rare plant grows in humid forests and beside rivers. It can be mistaken for cultivated grapevines that have escaped from old vineyards and returned to a more natural state, but the wild species' leaves are barely lobed, while cultivated grapevines have three or five distinct lobes. Another distinguishing feature is that the wild grape has separate male and female plants.

The plant clings to its supports by means of downy tendrils. Its brownish-grey bark changes over time as it comes off in small strips. The alternate leaves, which are downy on the underside, are heart-shaped at the base and divide into slight lobes with roughly dentate edges. The petiole is generally long (3–7 cm). Its many **flowers**, borne in panicles, consist of five greenish-yellow petals, measuring 4–5 mm and often fused at the top, forming a sort of hood that is later shed. Five prominent stamens emerge from each flower. Its **fruit** takes the form of round, purplish-blue grapes that are covered in a thin film of greyish bloom. They form hanging clusters.

Cultivated grape, flowers.

↕	5–10 m
✳	May/July
⚬⚬	September/November
▲▲	100–500 m
👄	Edible

Climbing Plants

Pampas lily of the valley, flowers.

PAMPAS LILY OF THE VALLEY

Salpichroa origanifolia · Solanaceae

Pampas lily of the valley,

Thanks to its impressive root system, this plant spreads farther each year into wild coastal heaths and areas with sandy soil. It is native to South America, but has adapted so well to some areas that efforts to control it are being considered. Nonetheless, it provides a late source of pollen for bees, flowering towards the end of summer.

The plant's hairy, climbing stems intermingle and give it a dense, branched appearance. Its oval, entire and alternate leaves (1–3.5 cm) taper to a point and are attached to the stems via a long petiole (8–16 mm). Single hanging **flowers** appear at the leaf joints. The flowers feature a small (10 mm), white, bell-shaped corolla made up of five petals which curve outwards, and a calyx of five pointed lobes. The stamens' converging anthers form a circle around the style. The shape, colour and size of its flower are reminiscent of the lily of the valley's bell-shaped flowers, hence its name. Its **fruit** takes the form of oval berries, about the size of a pigeon's egg (1.5–2 cm), which narrow to a point. The berries change colour from dark green to pale yellow as they ripen.

↕	1–3 m
☀	April/August
🍒	July/October
⛰	0–300 m
👄	Edible

Blue passion flower, flower.

Passiflora caerulea · Passifloraceae

This striking flower's unique appearance results from the intricate arrangement of its floral parts. It was discovered by the Jesuits, who named it passion flower as they thought its structure symbolized the death of Christ. The plant's large fruit are hard to miss, and their orange colour suggests an appetizing snack. This is misleading, as the tasty passion flower fruit in fact comes from other species – *P. edulis* and *P. incarnata*.

The plant, which has a climbing stem and branches that grip on to a support with small tendrils, grows in warm, sunny spots. Its leaves appear to be evergreen, but are eventually shed, typically from frost, as the plant is very sensitive to cold weather. Its leaves, which are divided into five lobes, come in different shapes. The plant's highly fragrant **flowers** are made up of a calyx of white, slightly tapering sepals, a corolla of five white petals topped with a crown of blue filaments, five greenish stamens with drooping anthers, and a pistil with three stigmas. It produces shiny, fleshy, orange-coloured accessory **fruit** with an elongated shape (2–4 cm).

Blue passion flower, fruit.

↕	3–10 m
✳	May/September
🍒	August/November
▲▲	0–600 m
✖	Inedible

Climbing Plants

Cornelian cherry, fruit.

TREE-LIKE SHRUBS WITH YELLOW, ORANGE, RED OR BROWN FRUIT

These plants have woody trunks and branches and resemble a small tree. They do not typically exceed 7 m in height. Their trunks are sometimes so short (1–3 cm above ground) that they look like bushes. However, the central axis defined by the trunk in the middle of the branches helps to identify them. In highland areas certain tree-like shrubs adapt to the harsh climate and develop a dwarf form (for example dwarf whitebeam).

Sea buckthorn, flowers.

SEA BUCKTHORN

Hippophae rhamnoides · Elaeagnaceae

Sea buckthorn, fruit.

This plant can be found in warm coastal areas of Europe and Asia but also survives in much cooler climates, including parts of coastal Britain and Russia, where it is called Siberian pineapple. In North America, where it grows only under cultivation, researchers are looking into the fruit's composition, as it contains 30 times more vitamin C than oranges. It is also a good source of B vitamins, trace elements, and saturated and unsaturated fatty acids. In light of the fruit's impressive nutritional profile, it is perhaps not surprising that it is used by athletes to improve their performance.

Sea buckthorn requires sun and light soil. It is most often found along streams, in alluvial zones, and on embankments and sand dunes. It is a dioecious species (male and female reproductive organs on separate plants) with deciduous leaves and silvery-scaled bark that is covered in many thorns. It features oblong, nearly sessile, entire leaves (4–6 cm) that form an alternate arrangement on its highly branched stems. The leaves are greyish on top and darker underneath. Its brownish, sessile **flowers**, which lack petals, form small catkins before the leaves appear. The male flowers are composed of four stamens and two sepals, while the female flowers have a single pistil and two small sepals. Its **fruit** takes the form of small, shiny, round, orange berries with an astringent flavour, which appear to be glued to the branches in tight clusters.

↕	3–5 m
✳	March/April
🍒	September/November
▲▲	0–1500 m
👄	Edible

RECIPE

SEA BUCKTHORN JELLY

Harvesting
Picking sea buckthorn berries is rather time-consuming.
Its fruit remain firmly attached to the branches, even when ripe. We have found that the best method is to use small scissors to cut off each berry individually from the shrub. Gloves should be worn to protect against the plant's thorns. When the fruit is fully ripe, one can also lay out a sheet at the foot of the shrub, shake the shrub and collect the fruit.

Ingredients
1 kg granulated sugar for 1 litre juice
Juice of 1 orange
Zest of lemon and orange

Method
Cover the berries with water in a saucepan and cook until they begin to break apart. Sieve the mixture and reserve the liquid. Squeeze the remaining pulp in a sieve to extract any remaining juice. Add this to the reserved liquid. Add an equal weight of sugar to this juice, as well as the orange juice and citrus zests. Return to the saucepan and cook the mixture until you obtain a jelly-like consistency.
Pour the jelly into jars and cover while it is still warm.

RECIPE

SEA BUCKTHORN JUICE

Therapeutic properties
The fruit's vitamin C content is among the highest observed. It also contains B vitamins, trace elements, anti-oxidants, silica, and flavonoids. The raw juice is an excellent tonic for temporary fatigue or as an annual health pick-me-up.

Method
Wash the berries and press them through a food mill with a fine sieve to extract the juice.
Dilute the juice by half with other fruit juices (for example orange or pineapple) to soften its acidity. Take one tablespoon of juice twice a day, morning and midday. Keep the juice refrigerated. The juice can be pasteurized, which allows it to be kept for several weeks. Many different types of prepared juices are available in the health food sections of chemists and other speciality shops.

Sea buckthorn, fruit.

Tree-like Shrubs with Yellow, Orange, Red or Brown Fruit

Strawberry tree, fruit.

STRAWBERRY TREE

Arbutus unedo · Ericaceae

Strawberry tree, flowers.

Often planted as a landscaping tree in the grounds of stately homes, the strawberry tree favours acid soils. It has many uses and is much loved by sculptors and wood turners. The fruit makes exquisite jams, jellies, syrups and liqueurs and can also be used as a preserve to accompany wild game.

The plant's twisted trunk is covered in reddish bark. Its leathery, oblong, alternate leaves remain on the branches for some time; they are glossy dark green, with dentate margins. The whitish, bell-shaped, hermaphroditic **flowers**, which are borne in drooping panicles of 10–25 from mid autumn to late winter, emit a pleasant fragrance. They are pitcher-shaped and the petals are sometimes green at the tips. The **fruit** takes the form of round berries resembling strawberries, changing colour from green, to yellow, to orange, and finally to red. They do not ripen until the following autumn, and thus are found alongside the new flowers.

↕	1–8 m
✴	October/January
☙	September/December (of the following year)
⛰	0–600 m
👄	Edible in small quantities

European red elder, flowers.

EUROPEAN RED ELDER

Sambucus racemosa · Caprifoliaceae

This elder's seeds are toxic and must be removed before consuming the fruit. This can be done by cooking the fruit for 15 minutes in a saucepan with a little water. Once the berries begin to burst, the juice is carefully sieved and used to make jellies and syrups. When distilled into a liqueur, it imparts a surprising, refined, and rather spicy taste. Found in northern Europe, this shrub was introduced as game cover in Britain (especially in Scotland).

The plant's curved branches have a brownish pith and their reddish bark is dotted with small grey bumps which are clearly visible. Its deciduous, opposite leaves are composed of 3–7 dentate, oval, pointed leaflets and are attached to the branches with long petioles. The profuse greenish-yellow **flowers**, with a five-lobed corolla, form large upright racemes at the end of the branches. The **fruit** takes the form of round, glossy, scarlet berries, 4–5 mm in diameter, containing three yellow flattened pips. The mature fruit clusters remain on the plant for a long period.

European red elder, fruit.

↕	2–3 m
☀	April/May
🍒	August/September
⛰	200–2000 m
👄	Fruit: edible if seeds are removed

Tree-like Shrubs with Yellow, Orange, Red or Brown Fruit

Cornelian cherry, flowers.

CORNELIAN CHERRY

Cornus mas · Cornaceae

Cornelian cherry, fruit.

The very hard wood of this plant was once used to craft the handles for tools and weapons as well as providing the key mechanical parts for mills and wine and cider presses. The plant's fruit can be turned into jams, preserved in salt and eaten like olives, or dried in the sun to be enjoyed as slightly tart sweets. This plant is regularly used in edible forest gardens.

The cornelian cherry's trunk is covered in brownish, scaly bark and its stems are dotted with opposite, warty buds. The entire, oval, opposite leaves are distinctly lighter underneath and end in a small point. Five to six pairs of curved, converging veins run through the leaf. As winter draws to a close and before the leaves emerge, many bright yellow **flowers** appear on its branches, borne in umbels supported by short stalks. Its **fruit** takes the form of oval drupes, which turn from green to orange and then a lovely bright red hue. They contain a large stone, resemble small elongated cherries and have a slightly tart flavour.

↕	3–6 m
✳	March/April
🍒	August/September
▲▲	0–1200 m
👄	Edible

Cornelian cherry, fruit.

RECIPE

CORNELIAN CHERRY JELLY

Harvesting
The cornelian cherry's fruit can be picked from late August to early
September, when it begins to turn red and fall to the ground. The shrub
can be shaken to encourage the fruit to drop.
The berries freeze well after they are washed.

Ingredients
1 kg sugar for 1 litre juice

Method
Carefully wash the fruit.
Use a juicer to extract the juice. Alternatively, place the fruit in a saucepan
and cover with water. Cook until the fruit begins to break apart. Pass the
liquid through a fine sieve. Pass the remaining pulp through a food mill in
small batches to extract as much pulp as possible. Be careful not to crush
the stones.
Press the pulp in a sieve to extract more juice and add it to the reserved
juice.
Weigh the juice and add an equal weight of sugar.
Cook the mixture until it reaches a jelly-like consistency.
Pour into jars and cover while still warm.

Goumi, flowers.

GOUMI

Elaeagnus multiflora · Elaeagnaceae

Goumi, fruit.

This rare species originating from China, Korea and Japan can be used to produce excellent wild fruit jams. It also makes an unusual wine, similar to redcurrant wine. It is a unique and special treat, which should be enjoyed in moderation.

The plant's many branches interweave to form a tufted bush, which provides hiding spots for wild animals. The whitish undersides of its semi-persistent leaves are punctuated with small brownish spots. Like the genus's other species, it has an abundance of fragrant **flowers**. The perianth is made up of four yellowish lobes which taper to a point, supported by very long peduncles. Its **fruit** takes the form of a small drupe which has a grainy surface and resembles an elongated cherry that hangs at the end of an extremely long stalk. The fruit's red colour can be seen from far away. Its flavour is close to that of the cornelian cherry: barely sweet, slightly tart, and slightly astringent.

↕	2–4 m
✺	April/May
⚭	Mid-July/Mid-August
⛰	200–600 m
👄	Edible

Wild Fruit

Common holly, male flowers.

Common holly, female flowers.

COMMON HOLLY

Ilex aquifolium · Aquifoliaceae

Birdlime was once extracted from holly by slicing the vascular tissues in its bark. This viscous substance was used to capture caterpillars and insects that would cause harm to grapevines. Unfortunately, birds are similarly trapped when they come into contact with the substance and the practice was eventually abandoned. The use of holly as a Christmas decoration still persists. However, one must keep a watchful eye on children, as its fruit and leaves contain toxic substances.

Holly can sometimes reach 10 m in height, resembling a small tree. A greenish-grey bark covers its hard and flexible wood. Its stiff, leathery, evergreen leaves have a waxy appearance and are spiny and dentate or entire without spines. White, pink-tinged **flowers** appear in small clusters at the base of the leaves. They are very small (5–7 mm) and are composed of 4–5 petals which are fused at the base. Common holly is a dioecious species, with male and female reproductive organs on separate plants. Its **fruit** takes the form of drupes, which mature from green to scarlet and last until the beginning of spring. The mature fruit are shiny and typically contain four triangular seeds.

Common holly, fruit.

↕	6–10 m
☀	May/June
🍒	November/March (of the following year)
▲▲	0–1800 m
🌿	Toxic

Cherry plum, flowers.

CHERRY PLUM

Prunus cerasifera · Rosaceae

Cherry plum, fruit.

As winter draws to a close, the cherry plum is one of first shrubs to flower in hedges, forest fringes and thickets. The plant is sometimes known as myrobalan plum, which derives from the same root as the mirabelle plum.

The colour of the branches is dark brown on the sides that are exposed to the light and light green on shaded parts. Its long (6–7 cm), deciduous, dentate leaves are lighter underneath and are attached to the branches via short petioles. Pure white **flowers** form shortly before the leaves appear. The flower's calyx is made up of sepals that curl backwards and its corolla consists of rounded petals that sit side-by-side. A single central pistil can be seen among the flower's many stamens. Its **fruit** takes the form of round drupes, which are roughly the size of a large cherry. They hang on short peduncles and take on a dark red colour when ripe. Somewhat tart flesh, which is barely palatable, surround the smooth stone. They become slightly more flavourful when cooked.

↕	6–8 m
✳	March/April
🍒	July/September
▲▲	100–700 m
👄	Edible, though not very palatable

Sour cherry, flowers.

SOUR CHERRY

Prunus cerasus · Rosaceae

The dried stems of this plant's fruit can be prepared as a herb tea or decocted into medicinal preparations, employed for their diuretic and cleansing properties. The stems are also pulverized to a fine powder and administered in capsule form. Their chief active ingredients are potassium salts and tannins.

The plant's thin branches, which sprawl or droop slightly, bear thick, shiny leaves, which feel rough. Before the leaves appear, white **flowers** made up of nearly circular petals form small clusters on its branches. A few brownish scales surround the base of the flowers' long peduncles. The plant's **fruit** takes the form of a shiny, bright red drupe, which has a slight depression at the tip. The somewhat tart flesh does not attach to the stone. This plant is also commonly known as tart cherry and wild cherry.

Sour cherry, fruit.

↕	3–6 m
✳	April/May
🍒	July/August
▲▲	0–1200 m
👄	Edible

Guelder rose, flowers.

GUELDER ROSE

Viburnum opulus · Caprifoliaceae

Guelder rose, fruit

The attractive drupes of the guelder rose usually remain on the plant for some time as birds pay little attention to them until other food sources become scarce, when bullfinches and thrushes begin to consume them in large quantities. Horticulturists have created ornamental cultivars from the plant, among them the celebrated snowball tree (*V. opulus* 'Roseum'), with its exquisite flower clusters.

Guelder rose is native to Europe, north Africa and central Asia and has naturalized in North America. The young branches initially grow upright and then begin to curve. Many raised pores punctuate their light brown bark. The opposite leaves, which are divided into three uneven lobes, are roughly dentate. The undersides of the leaves are covered in a thin layer of matted woolly down. The **flowers** form spreading corymbs (6–10 cm), the inner flowers small and yellowish, while the white outer flowers are larger, sterile, and made up of uneven petals. The **toxic** fruit takes the form of shiny, bright red, spherical drupes (8–9 mm), each of which contains a single stone. They cause serious intestinal troubles when eaten raw or in large quantities and are sometimes mistaken for redcurrants by children. However, the drupes' bitter flavour tends to limit their consumption.

↕	2–4 m
✳	May/July
🍒	September/October
▲▲	0–1400 m
☠	Toxic

Almond, flowers.

ALMOND

Prunus dulcis · Rosaceae

Almond, fruits.

This tree's early blossom graces the countryside of mainland Europe as winter draws to a close, when white flowers with red centres smother the crown. The foliage appears later. The almonds produced can be bitter or sweet, depending on the plant's particular variety: *P. dulcis* var. *amara* contains a bitter substance, while *P. dulcis* var. *sativa* produces the sweet almond that is used in various ways.

The plant's many branches initially grow upright but spread over time. Its long, deciduous, lance-shaped leaves are glossy and dentate, with short petioles and a clearly visible primary vein. Pink or white, nearly sessile **flowers** appear on its branches. They have a bell-shaped calyx, a corolla with large, jagged petals, and numerous (20–30) stamens. The **fruit** takes the form of greenish, oval, velvety, pointed drupes containing a stone inside of which resides an edible bitter or sweet almond.

↕	5–8 m
☀	Mid-February/March
♠♠	September/October
▲▲	0–1000 m
👄	Edible

Tree-like Shrubs with Yellow, Orange, Red or Brown Fruit

Azarole, flowers (buds).

AZAROLE

Crataegus azarolus · Rosaceae

Azarole, fruit.

This tree certainly lives up to the old adage 'slowly but surely', as the first harvest only takes place after ten years of growth. However, once it reaches that point the azarole will reward with repeated harvests for a long period of time, as it is exceptionally long-lived, generally from five to six centuries. Ancient trees may have a trunk exceeding 2 m in circumference. The azarole generally grows in the Mediterranean region and is not found wild in Britain.

Its straight, somewhat spiny trunk is topped by a dense, rounded crown. The bark starts to crack with age and the down that covers the young branches begins to fade. The alternate leaves, with three or five lobes, have a characteristic shape that resembles a goose's foot. They are hairy underneath, as are the small petioles that support them, and slightly glossy on top. The fragrant white **flowers** consist of many pink stamens, two styles, a hairy calyx, and a five-petalled corolla. They are followed by shiny, oval accessory **fruit** of 1–2 cm in diameter with thin skin and up to five stones. The colour varies from red to orange-yellow. The slightly tart flesh fruit can be eaten raw or stewed, or turned into jam or liqueurs.

↕	2–10 m
✳	April–May
🍒	September
▲▲	0–400 m
👄	Edible

Common hawthorn, fruit.

Common hawthorn, flowers.

COMMON HAWTHORN

Crataegus monogyna · Rosaceae

This plant is also commonly known as may and hedgerow thorn. Its flowering tops are used medicinally for their regulating and sedative properties. Its berries, known as haws, can be turned into delicious jellies and marmalades. A delicious ketchup can also be made using the deseeded berries instead of tomatoes.

The plant's long-lived branches have grey bark and are very spiny. Its smooth, glossy, alternate leaves are darker on the underside and are generally divided into five or seven lobes by deep indentations. A number of rather foul-smelling, white, sometimes pinkish **flowers** appear in clusters on the plant. A single style can be found at the centre of the rounded petals. The bright red, nearly round **fruit** measures 5–10 mm and contains a single stone. The plant is chiefly found along hedges and the fringes of open, sunny forests.

Crataegus curvisepala, leaves and fruit.

↕	6–8 m
✺	April/June
🍒	August/November
▲▲	0–1600 m
👄	Fruit: edible, flower: for medicinal use

Tree-like Shrubs with Yellow, Orange, Red or Brown Fruit

Midland hawthorn, flowers.

MIDLAND HAWTHORN

Crataegus laevigata · Rosaceae

Midland hawthorn, fruit.

Crataegus laevigata subsp. *palmstruchii*, fruit.

This species has another botanical name, *Crataegus oxyacantha*. Unlike the closely related common hawthorn, which prefers forest edges and roadsides, the midland hawthorn favours open woodland. Passerine birds are very fond of the fruit of both hawthorn species. The hawfinch is one of the few birds which is able to break the fruit's stone, on account of its powerful beak.

The plant's spiny, alternate leaves are light green on top and their petioles are hairless. The leaves are oval at the base and rounded at the tip, with slight lobes. At the end of winter, the shrub is covered in single or clustered white **flowers**, which are punctuated by the reddish spots of the anthers. On each flower, two to three styles can be observed. The plant produces many bright red, nearly spherical **fruit**, known as haws, which measure 8–12 mm in diameter. Each haw contains 2–3 small stones of varying sizes.

DID YOU KNOW?

Crataegus laevigata subsp. *palmstruchii*
The plant's sepals are twice as long as they are wide. Its fruit measures 10–16 mm.
Crataegus × media
This hybrid between *C. monogyna* and *C. laevigata* features leaves that come in different shapes and its flowers may be different colours.

～

↕	2–4 m
☀	April/June
🍒	August/November
⛰	100–1500 m
👄	Edible

Wild Fruit

RECIPE

HAWTHORN JELLY

Harvesting
The fruit can be picked once the flesh begins to soften.
Mind the thorns!

Method
Wash the fruit and remove any remaining peduncles. Place in a large saucepan
and cover with water.
Cook until the fruit can be easily be crushed with a wooden spoon.
Sieve the mixture and reserve the juice.
Gather the remaining fruit and press it in the sieve to extract the remaining juice.
Add this to the reserved juice.
Weigh the juice and add an equivalent weight of granulated sugar.
Allow to sit for 2–3 hours. Cook the mixture until it forms a jelly.
Pour into jars and cover while warm.

RECIPE

HAWTHORN TEA

Background
The floral parts of the midland hawthorn and common hawthorn can both be
used, as well as the leaves and fruit. All contain the same active ingredients. The
best time to harvest them is at flowering time.

Therapeutic properties
Hawthorn is a heart tonic, which helps to regulate rhythm and blood pressure.
It also has sedative and calming properties that can soothe anxiety and nerves.

Method and directions for use
Pour boiling water over 5–10 g of dried plant material in a large cup. Allow to steep
for 10 minutes. Follow a course of treatment of 2 cups per day over 2–3 weeks.

Crataegus × media, flowers.

Spindle, flowers.

Spindle, white-fruited variety.

SPINDLE

Euonymus europaeus · Celastraceae

Spindle, fruit.

The wood of this tree is carbonized in a vacuum to make artists' charcoal. Its texture can be hard or soft, depending on the manufacturing process. Its use goes back to the Stone Age, when it was employed to create cave drawings that are still visible today. The tree's many other common names include catwood, pegwood, prickwood, prick timber and skewerwood. It is native across Europe.

The plant's young greenish-grey branches are initially ribbed but become smooth. Its opposite, oval leaves, which are 3–4 cm in length, come to a point. They have finely dentate edges and short petioles. Its inconspicuous whitish-green **flowers** (9–10 mm), borne in compound cymes, are composed of four separate petals in a cross shape and prominent stamens. The plant's characteristic **fruit** takes the form of a reddish-pink capsule, which contains four small fleshy orange sacs that house the seeds. Like the rest of the plant, they are toxic.

↕	4–5 m
☀	April/June
☙	September/November
▲▲	0–700 m
☠	Toxic

DID YOU KNOW?

Euonymus europaeus f. *alba*
The fruit's capsule remains white.

∿∿

Large-leaved spindle, flowers.

LARGE-LEAVED SPINDLE

Euonymus latifolia · Celastraceae

According to some experts, if global warming continues unimpeded, our landscapes will be transformed. Southern species will progressively expand their ranges and the lower strata of mountain vegetation will also look very different from how it does today. The large-leaved spindle, which is already quite sparsely distributed, will become even less numerous due to competition. It can currently be found at higher altitudes in mainland Europe, in open woods, along roadsides, and in partially shaded areas. It is often found in the company of terrestrial orchids and Italian maples.

The plant's rather slender, round young stems divide into reddish-brown branches. Its very large deciduous leaves are 8–10 cm long, 4–5 cm wide, and come to a point. The leaves are opposite and have very short petioles (less than 1 cm). The small, pinkish-green **flowers** are clustered in cymes that hang on long pedicels. The five petals of the flower's corolla form a star. Its **fruit** takes the form of a dark red capsule, which opens up widely at maturity to expose five fleshy orange envelopes, each containing a single large seed. The entire plant is toxic.

Large-leaved spindle, fruit.

↕	2–4 m
✳	May/June
🍒	September/October
▲▲	600–1800 m
☠	Toxic

Dwarf whitebeam, flowers.

Dwarf whitebeam, fruit.

DWARF WHITEBEAM

Sorbus chamaemespilus · Rosaceae

Sorbus ambigua, fruit.

This plant grows only at high altitudes in mainland Europe, mainly in subalpine habitats, just below the tree line. Also known as false medlar, it prefers full sun or part shade. It is considered a pioneer species, which can easily establish itself and tolerate difficult weather conditions. Individual plants are sometimes found among bilberries, cotoneasters and other *Sorbus* species.

The plant's thick branches are covered in brown bark which is punctuated by raised pores. Its entire, alternate leaves are tightly packed and have tiny petioles. The leaves are oval, 4–8 cm long and glossy on top with a doubly dentate edge, except towards the base. Clusters of white or light pink **flowers** form at the ends of the branches, borne in corymbs. At the centre of their downy sepals and stamens, two styles are visible. The accessory **fruit** mature from lemon-yellow to orange-red, with a diameter of 10–12 mm and the remains of the calyx visible at the end. They have a floury texture and a tart flavour.

↕	0.5–1 m
✳	June/July
◌	September
▲▲	700–2500 m
〰	Edible

DID YOU KNOW?

Sorbus ambigua
This hybrid between *Sorbus chamaemespilus* and *Sorbus aria* is of an average height (up to 3 m). Its fruit are red.

〜〜

Wild Fruit

Mougeot's whitebeam, flowers.

MOUGEOT'S WHITEBEAM

Sorbus mougeotii · Rosaceae

The different species of the genus *Sorbus* tend to hybridize with one another, which often results in sterile specimens. There are some exceptions, as certain hybrids can reproduce by apomixis, a sort of natural cloning. Such is the case with the Mougeot's whitebeam, which makes use of this reproductive technique that does not require fertilization. These apomictic species created through asexual reproduction are in fact microspecies. They were discovered by the French physician Jean-Antoine Mougeot, who had a passion for botany.

The plant's trunk is sometimes small and supports elongated branches that are curved and covered in a reddish bark dotted by long raised pores. The leaves are slightly lobed, with undulate edges and clearly visible veins. They are quite large – 8–10 cm long and 3–5 cm wide – with a light green upper surface that and contrasts with the underside, which is hairy and whitish. The **flowers** have a white corolla, long petals and two fused styles surrounded by large stamens, and form evenly distributed clusters. The glossy bright red accessory **fruit**, produced in small clusters at the ends of the stems, are nearly round. They have a mildly bitter flavour.

Mougeot's whitebeam, fruit.

↕	4–6 m
☀	May/June
🍒	August/September
▲▲	500–2000 m
🐾	Unpalatable

Pomegranate, flowers.

POMEGRANATE

Punica granatum · Lythraceae

Pomegranate, fruit.

To make true grenadine syrup, the pulp from the pomegranate's fruit must be removed, juiced, and sieved, to which an equal weight of sugar is added. The mixture is then brought to a boil and cooked until the liquid forms 2–3 cm strands as it runs off a spatula. It is then allowed to cool and kept refrigerated. The naturally derived syrups differ from their artificial counterparts by the presence of flavonoid pigments known as anthocyanins. The other syrups are made from red colourings.

Commonly used as an ornamental garden plant, the pomegranate has somewhat thorny angular stems. Its smooth, glossy, entire, opposite leaves (5–8 cm) are veined and have rather short petioles. Scarlet sessile **flowers** measuring 4–5 cm in diameter are found singly or in groups of two or three at the ends of the branches. The flower's fleshy calyx forms a tube which ends in 7–8 lobes and its corolla is composed of five or more ruffled petals, inside of which are a number of stamens that surround a single style. Its **fruit** is the pomegranate, which is a false fruit that results from the swelling of the flower's calyx. Nearly round, it is topped by the remains of the flower's sepals and can vary from yellowish-green to reddish-brown in colour. Inside the fruit, partitions separate the many seeds which are surrounded by a gelatinous, edible, orange-red pulp, with a sour flavour.

↕	4–6 m
✺	June/July
🍒	October/November
⛰	0–500 m
👄	Edible

Quince, flower.

Quince, fruit.

QUINCE

Cydonia oblonga · Rosaceae

The fruit of the quince is used for jellies, compotes, fruit pastes, syrups, liqueurs, and brandies. In ancient civilizations, the seeds were made into a jelly that was applied externally to smooth and set hair. Quince grows wild in warmer parts of Europe and as a garden plant elsewhere. The fruits are hard to find, as they are often stripped from the tree soon after reaching a good size and sold at inflated prices.

The plant's sprawling young branches have a brownish bark that is covered in fine, short hairs. Its fairly large (4–8 cm), oval, alternate leaves are whitish and hairy underneath. Large, white, single **flowers** veined with pink are borne at the ends of the branches. The calyx is composed of sepals dotted with glands that secrete fragrant oils, while the corolla has curved petals. Five fused styles sit at the centre of numerous stamens. The yellowish **fruit**, the quince, is in the shape of a pear or apple and has a characteristic fragrance when ripe. A fine down covers the surface. Its hard flesh is rich in pectin and is divided into five sections which contain several pips. It has an astringent taste.

RECIPE

QUINCE PASTE

Harvesting
The fragrant fruit can be picked in October.

Ingredients
Equal weights of fruit and granulated sugar

Method
Scrub the fruit to remove the down on the surface. Cut it into quarters and remove the pips. Slice the fruit, place in a saucepan and leave for roughly an hour to allow it to soften. The juice can be used to make jelly. Pass the remaining flesh through a food mill. The pulp obtained will be used to make the fruit paste. Add an equal weight of sugar to the pulp and cook until it forms a smooth paste that is easily scraped from the sides of the pan. Spread out the mixture in a 1 cm layer. Allow to dry for several days and cut into small squares. Store in a metal tin with each layer carefully separated by sheets of greaseproof paper.

↕	4–6 m
☀	April/May
🍒	Mid-September/November
⛰	0–800 m
👄	Edible

Tree-like Shrubs with Yellow, Orange, Red or Brown Fruit

Crab apple, flowers.

Crab apple, leaves and flowers.

CRAB APPLE

Malus sylvestris · Rosaceae

Crab apple, fruit.

There is no shortage of apple varieties and telling them apart can sometimes prove difficult. To simplify things, apples are classed into three categories: the wild species, cultivated varieties and naturalized apple trees. *Malus sylvestris*, a wild species, is used as stocks for grafting with cultivated apple varieties. The wood is also used to make sculptures and various artefacts.

The crab apple has slightly thorny branches with greyish-brown bark that becomes cracked and scaly. Its oval, dentate leaves have 3–4 pairs of veins running through them and are attached to the branches via a short petiole. They are initially downy and become smooth with time. The **flower**'s corolla, which is white on the inside and scarlet-tinged outside, surrounds yellowish stamens. The flowers release a pleasant fragrance and are arranged in corymbs, in what is one of the most attractive spring flower displays. This species bears a rather modest-sized (3–5 cm), greenish-yellow accessory **fruit** with red spots. It has a hard pulp and a bitter taste.

↕	5–7 m
☀	April/May
⚬⚬	August/October
▲▲	0–1200 m
✺	Unpalatable

Almond-leaved pear, flowers.

Pyrus spinosa · Rosaceae

Unlike other pear species, the almond-leaved pear can grow in warm habitats, under dry conditions, and in poor soil. It is usually found alongside Italian buckthorn, olive trees, mastic trees and almonds in southern Europe (occasionally as a garden plant elsewhere). These species are all important constituents of mixed hedges, which contribute to maintaining biodiversity and limiting soil erosion.

Its sturdy, straight, long branches are dotted with many thorns. The simple, entire, alternate leaves (5–7 cm) are at least twice as long as they are wide. They are glossy on top and covered with downy whitish hairs underneath. More than seven pairs of veins are clearly visible on the surface. The plant's white **flowers**, which form corymbs, are made up of five petals that are fused at the base with the calyx's five sepals. The stamens have pinkish-purple anthers. Its **fruit** takes the form of a roundish, greenish-brown pear, which is roughly 3–4 cm in diameter. The fruit has granular, bitter-tasting flesh and is inedible.

Almond-leaved pear, fruit.

↕	4–6 m
✳	April/May
🍒	September
⛰	0–1500 m
🐾	Unpalatable

Tree-like Shrubs with Yellow, Orange, Red or Brown Fruit

Wild pear, flowers.

WILD PEAR

Pyrus pyraster · Rosaceae

Wild pear, fruit.

This widespread solitary species is often confused with *Pyrus communis*, which is also known as the wild pear. It has a long history as a pioneer plant and is thought to be the ancestor of all cultivated species of pears developed through selective breeding or through crossing with Asian pears. Pliny the Elder enumerates close to 40 varieties, and nowadays there are more varieties than can easily be counted.

The tree's long branches are somewhat thorny, with brown or grey bark that becomes scaly with time. Its slightly dentate leaves, with petioles as long as the blades, are glossy on top and duller underneath. The plant produces many spring **flowers** that form small clusters. The flowers have rounded, white petals, stamens topped with scarlet red anthers, and free-standing styles. The **fruit** takes the form of small yellowish-green pears, which have the remains of the calyx on the end. They ripen in late autumn, though their flesh remains hard and bitter until it is bletted.

↕	4–10 m
☀	April/May
♠	August/September
▲▲	0–1100 m
✖	Unpalatable

DID YOU KNOW?

Plymouth pear – *Pyrus cordata*
The petioles of the plant's heart-shaped leaves are longer than the leaf blades. The reddish fruit is scattered with small scales and bears no visible remains of the flower.

Snow pear – *Pyrus nivalis*
The plant's hairy leaves have distinct veins running through them. Its flowers have hairy styles.

∿

Plymouth pear, fruit.

Plymouth pear, flowers.

Snow pear, unripe fruit.

Common medlar, flower.

COMMON MEDLAR

Mespilus germanica · Rosaceae

Common medlar, fruit.

As the tree is a native of southwest Asia and southeast Europe, the fruit of the medlar struggles to ripen fully in cooler climates, such as that of Britain. However, it can be left to blet for a few weeks and once bletted, it can be made into a delicious chocolate and medlar pudding.

The plant's slightly thorny branches grow slowly. Its deciduous, alternate leaves are of a fair size, measuring 10–12 cm in length and 2–4 cm in width. The leaves are matt on top, while their undersides are covered in a layer of woolly down. A single **flower** forms at the end of each branch. The flowers have white, rounded, undulating petals which are fairly long (4 cm), and a number of stamens with red anthers surround five styles, arranged in a star shape. The average-sized **fruit**, known as medlar, are slightly hairy, and turn from their initial green colour to a coppery hue, finally becoming dark brown. The remains of the flower's calyx forms a crown around a small cavity at the tip of the fruit. After the first frosts, the fruit's flesh becomes overripe, at which point it can be eaten.

↕	2–4 m
☀	May/June
🍒	October/November
⛰	0–1000 m
👄	Edible

DID YOU KNOW?

Crataegomespilus dardarii, a hybrid of medlar and hawthorn, was developed by a French horticulturist named Dardar.

〜〜

RECILE

RECIPE

MEDLAR JAM

Harvesting
Medlar fruit are edible only after the first frosts.
They can be picked earlier and stored in straw or newspaper until they fully
soften.

Ingredients
750 g granulated sugar for 1 kg fruit purée

Method
Quarter the medlars and remove the seeds. Place in a large saucepan
and cover with water. Bring the mixture to a boil and allow to cook for 15
minutes. Purée the fruit by passing it through a food mill with a fine sieve.
Weigh the mixture and add the sugar. Return to the saucepan and cook on
low heat, stirring continuously, for 15 minutes.
Pour into jars and cover with lids.

RECIPE

MEDLAR FRUIT PASTE

Harvesting
Pick the fruit when they are overripe.

Ingredients
Equal weights of granulated sugar and pulp

Method
Refer to the instructions for the jam recipe above.
In a saucepan, add the sugar to the remaining pulp and cook the mixture.
Stir continuously until the mass detaches from the sides of the saucepan.
Cover a plate or a tray with greaseproof paper and sprinkle with sugar.
Spread a 1 cm thick layer of the mixture on top and sprinkle with sugar
once again.
Allow to dry for several days before slicing it into small squares.
Carefully place them in a metal tin, separating each layer with a sheet of
greaseproof paper.

Medlar, fruit (late autumn).

Tree-like Shrubs with Yellow, Orange, Red or Brown Fruit

Large-fruited variety of prickly juniper, fruit.

PRICKLY JUNIPER

Juniperus oxycedrus · Cupressaceae

Prickly juniper, fruit.

This plant is known by a number of other common names, including prickly cedar, cade juniper, or even just cade. When wandering about the Mediterranean hinterland (it rarely grows elsewhere), one can stumble on old cade ovens which have been restored. The concept is simple. Inside, the wood burns slowly, and the oil is collected in the lower part. This was once a widespread artisanal way of producing cade oil in the fields.

The plant's small, straight, needle-shaped evergreen leaves are in whorls of three. The top of the leaf is demarcated by a central vein that separates it into whitish strips, while its underside forms a keel-shaped structure along its centre. The inconspicuous female **flowers** take the form of greenish cones, while its male flowers have a more yellowish colour. The male and female flowers are found on separate plants. Its **fruit** takes the form of a galbulus, which is light green the first year and becomes reddish-brown. The fruit is 8–10 mm in size and contains an angular seed.

↕	2–8 m
☀	April/May
🝆	August/October
⛰	0–1200 m
🗱	Unpalatable

DID YOU KNOW?

J. oxycedrus subsp. *macrocarpa*
The plant's fruit are distinctly larger. It is a
protected species in some areas.

∽

Phoenicean juniper, shrub.

Phoenicean juniper, leaves and fruit.

PHOENICEAN JUNIPER

Juniperus phoenicea · Cupressaceae

This juniper is said to be among the xerophile plant species (adapted to grow and reproduce with a limited availability of water). This drought tolerance allows it to colonize very dry, sunny spots. It shows a preference for chalky soil, and can be found on ledges, cliffs, dry slopes, rocky ground, and stony heaths in southern Europe.

The Phoenicean juniper is a small, dense, cone-shaped shrub. Its trunk has greyish bark and bears relatively dense branches. Its leaves are reduced to small green scales, which are highly interwoven and arranged in six rows. On the older leaves, the central part is bordered by darker strips. The female **flowers** form round masses at the base of the leaves, while the inconspicuous cones of its male flowers are on other branches. Its **fruit** takes the form of a shiny false berry (7–10 mm), known as a galbulus, which is brownish-green the first year and turns a crimson-brown colour the following year. The fruit contains 7–10 seeds.

Phoenicean juniper, fruit.

↕	3–6 m
☀	March/April
🍒	August/September
▲▲	0–1000 m
☠	Toxic

Tree-like Shrubs with Yellow, Orange, Red or Brown Fruit

Common myrtle, fruit.

TREE-LIKE SHRUBS WITH BLUISH-BLACK FRUIT

These plants have woody trunks and branches and resemble a small tree. They do not typically exceed 7 m in height. Their trunks are sometimes so short (1–3 cm above ground) that they resemble bushes. However, the central axis defined by the trunk in the middle of the branches helps in their identification. In upland areas certain tree-like shrubs adapt to the harsh climate and develop a dwarf form.

Snowy mespilus, flowers.

SNOWY MESPILUS

Amelanchier ovalis · Rosaceae

Snowy mespilus, fruit.

Amelanchier ovalis subsp. *embergeri*, leaves.

This bold plant colonizes some of the highest possible sites, including ledges, rocky ridges and crevices, but can also be found on grassy patches, rocky slopes, open woods and scrub. As if to draw more attention to itself, it produces an abundance of flowers followed by a vast number of tasty fruit.

The plant's trunk is covered in a greyish bark and is somewhat branched. Its oval, alternate, dentate, light green leaves are hairless on top and crisscrossed with whitish veins. The undersides of the leaves are covered in a cottony down which disappears gradually. A large number of white **flowers** appear on its branches. The flowers consist of long, narrow, spaced petals, and a small calyx covered in a woolly down. It bears average-sized (5–7 mm), round, blackish-blue accessory **fruit**, which appear very early and have a pleasant flavour. The star-shaped remains of the flower's calyx are visible at the tip of the fruit.

↕	1–3 m
✺	April/May
🍒	June/August
⛰	0–1700 m
👄	Edible

DID YOU KNOW?

Amelanchier ovalis subsp. *embergeri*
The plant's dark green leaves have clearly dentate margins and its fruit are larger.

∿

Wild Fruit

Bay tree, flowers.

Laurus nobilis · Lauraceae

The fruit of the bay tree was once used to make an ointment to treat tender joints and sprains. Oil obtained from the fruit also serves as an insect repellent to keep mosquitoes at bay. The oil is obtained by crushing and straining the fruit and then heating it. The extracted oil is then dried and mixed with beeswax or lard. To keep insects away, spread the ointment on exposed skin. The plant is found in its largest numbers around the Mediterranean coast but it is a popular garden plant and grows well in southern England.

The bay tree's blackish-grey trunk splits into many branches that release a lovely aromatic fragrance. Its fairly thick, evergreen leaves are widely used in cookery. They are lance-shaped (5–12 cm), with undulate edges, and are glossy on top and glandular underneath. Its many fragrant, yellowish **flowers** form at the leaf joints. It is a dioecious species, with male and female reproductive organs on separate plants. The male flowers have many stamens (10–12) and the female flowers have a short, broad style. The **fruit** takes the form of a shiny, oval, black drupe, which can reach 2 cm in length and contains a single stone.

Bay tree, fruit.

↕	2–8 m
☀	March/May
◇◇	August/September
▲▲	0–600 m
〰	Edible

Oregon grape, flowers.

OREGON GRAPE

Mahonia aquifolium · Berberidaceae

Oregon grape, fruit.

This plant has come up with an effective strategy to ensure that its pollen is transported by insects – as soon as the insect brushes against the base of its stamens, they suddenly curl up round it. The surprised forager cannot make the slightest movement to free itself and its entire body becomes covered in pollen.

Native to North America, Oregon grape grows abundantly on the west coast and to a lesser extent on the east. In the rest of the world, the plant has become naturalized in many areas. Its brownish-grey stems bear glossy, spiny, alternate, evergreen leaves. They are light green underneath and are divided into 5–9 leaflets, which lack petioles save for the terminal leaflet. In winter, the leaves take on a lovely shade of reddish-brown. The many fragrant, yellow **flowers** form imposing panicles (6–10 cm), the corollas consisting of rounded petals, arranged in two concentric circles around six stamens which are loaded with pollen. The **fruit** take the form of elongated, bluish berries covered in a thin bloom. The dark purple flesh has a bitter taste.

	1–1.5 m
☀	March/April
🍒	July/October
⛰	0–1200 m
☠	Slightly toxic (seeds)

Common myrtle, flowers.

Myrtus communis · Myrtaceae

Common myrtle, fruit.

Myrtle has been associated with the goddess Venus since Greco-Roman antiquity on account of its strong fragrance, which is said to make people fall in love and to keep love alive. This idea seems still to prevail, as its fruit is distilled to this day to obtain a perfumed liquid known as *eau d'ange*, or 'angel water'. When applied regularly, it is said to preserve a fresh, youthful complexion. The plant has yet more uses: its essential oil is employed as an antiseptic for airways, and it is used in cookery to flavour roasts and steaks, and occasionally as a substitute for pepper. For those who enjoy spirits, soaking its berries yields an excellent liqueur.

At first upright, the plant begins to curve with age. Its angular, thornless branches have reddish bark and form dense bushes. When bruised, its leathery, evergreen leaves release a fragrance. They are nearly sessile, lance-shaped and opposite. Whitish **flowers** that smell of camphor are supported by long pedicels at the leaf joints. The sepals that make up the flower's calyx are covered in delicate hairs and combine to form a tube, while the petals that surround the bouquet of stamens remain separate from one another. The **fruit** take the form of small, slightly fleshy, bluish-black berries which are covered in a bloom and bear the remains of the flower's calyx at their ends.

↕	2–3 m
✳	May/July
🫐	August/September
⛰	0–400 m
👄	Edible

Tree-like Shrubs with Bluish-black Fruit

Common elder, flowers

Common elder, green-fruited variety.

COMMON ELDER

Sambucus nigra · Caprifoliaceae

Common elder, fruit.

The fruit of the common elder can be turned into jam, ketchup and wine, while its flower-heads make delicious fritters. Its other common names include black elder, pipe tree, and bore tree. Since the dawn of time, its bark, leaves, flowers and fruit have been used for their medicinal properties. Juice obtained from its fruit was also used as a food colouring to mark meat.

The plant's pliable stems are covered in a warty greyish bark and have a white pith which becomes yellowish with time. On its younger branches, a number of grey outgrowths can be observed. The asymmetrical leaves are made up of 5–7 oval dentate leaflets carried by a small petiole (2–3 cm). The plant produces an abundance of **flowers** which give off a characteristic, mildly pleasing aroma. These have a white corolla with five small, blunt-tipped petals (2–4 mm) which are fused and spread widely. The stamens are topped with pale yellow anthers. The **fruit** takes the form of round black berries, which have purple juice and hang in clusters from long purplish-red pedicels.

↕	3–7 m
✱	June/July
🍒	September/Mid-October
⛰	0–1500 m
👄	Edible

DID YOU KNOW?

Sambucus nigra var. *viridis*
The plant's ripe fruit keep their green colour.

〜

RECIPE

ELDERFLOWER FRITTERS

Harvesting
Cut the flowers when they reach maturity in June.

Ingredients
Common elder flowerheads (including stalks)
Icing sugar
Batter:
200 g sifted flour
half a glass of water
5 ml elderflower liqueur
2 tablespoons olive oil
pinch of salt
1 egg yolk
oil for frying

Method
Remove any debris from the flowerheads, wash them and allow to drain.
Make a well in the flour and pour in the water, liqueur, oil, salt, and egg yolk.
Mix well with a whisk. Sieve the mixture if there are lumps.
Carefully dip the flowerheads in the batter and drop them into the hot oil.
Allow to fry until golden.
Serve with a dusting of icing sugar.

RECIPE

ELDERBERRY JELLY

Harvesting
The fruit fully ripen in September.
Cut the berry clusters off the plant and discard any green berries.
Place the fruit in a bucket as it stains easily.

Ingredients
1 kg sugar for 1 kg of juice
1 lemon

Method
Picking the berries off the stems is tedious work, though you can save time by
passing a fork through the clusters to remove them. Wash the fruit.
The juice can be extracted with a juicer. Alternatively, the berries can be heated in
a saucepan until they burst, and the juice strained. If using this method, press the
remaining fruit in a sieve to extract even more juice. Weigh the juice and add an
equal weight of sugar. Add the juice of the lemon.
Cook on low heat in a saucepan for half an hour. Stir the mixture regularly
and skim off any foam that forms on the surface. Check to see if the jelly has
reached the setting point by dribbling a few drops on a chilled plate. If they set
immediately, the jelly is ready.
Pour into jars and cover.

Common dogwood, flowers.

COMMON DOGWOOD

Cornus sanguinea · Cornaceae

Common dogwood, fruit.

After it has shed the last of its leaves, the plant's wine-coloured branches stand out against the surrounding landscape. Its bark produces red sap which allows the plant to absorb more light in winter, an adaption which seems to have served it well, as the species spreads quickly and can become invasive. Its fruit were once used to produce lamp oil.

This plant puts out lots of stems and readily produces suckers. Its branches, which are green at first, take on an attractive wine-crimson colour in winter. The entire, opposite, pointed oval leaves are hairy underneath and have 3–4 pairs of primary veins running through them. They take on a reddish-brown tinge in autumn. The white **flowers**, which have narrow petals and prominent stamens, form corymbs and give off an unpleasant odour. The **fruit** takes the form of small, round, blackish-blue drupes whose surface is punctuated with small grey points. They are toxic and have a bitter taste.

↕	1.2–4m
✱	May/June
🍒	September/October
▲▲	0–1400 m
✖	Toxic

Alder buckthorn, flowers.

Alder buckthorn, fruit.

Frangula alnus · Rhamnaceae

Also known as black alder, this plant can adapt well to both damp and dryer areas. Different parts of the plant have been put to use in various ways. Fragments of the inner bark, dried for a year, were traditionally used for their laxative properties, and the pulverized charcoal obtained from its wood was used to manufacture cannon powder. Extreme caution should be taken when using the bark as it can be violently purgative – it should not be taken regularly by anyone or at all by people with bowel problems.

The characteristic bark of this thornless plant is punctuated with grey raised pores. Its many supple, long branches are arranged alternately. It has smooth-edged, entire, alternate leaves that get wider towards the upper third of the blade. On the undersides of the leaves, 7–9 pairs of prominent veins are visible. Its rather inconspicuous whitish **flowers** (2–3 mm) form small bunches at the leaf joints and give off a foul odour. Its **fruit** takes the form of berries, which turn from green to red and finally to black, and are between 5–8 mm in diameter.

RECIPE

═══ ALDER ═══ BUCKTHORN TEA

Harvesting
The plant's bark is used to prepare the tea. Harvest the bark in autumn. We recommend using a tool in the shape of a small scraper to remove the bark, in order to not damage the shrub. The bark scrapings must then be dried for a year to allow the irritant compounds found within it to fully break down.

Therapeutic properties
The main active compounds have a laxative effect. It is also beneficial in draining bile to the intestine.

Method and directions for use
Use a small teaspoon of crushed bark (pre-made preparations are available) for one cup of boiling water.
Allow to steep for 10 minutes. This treatment must only be used occasionally. Regular use is not recommended.
Do not administer to children.

↕	2–5 m
☀	May/July
🍒	August/Mid-October
⛰	0–1100 m
✗	Unpalatable

Tree-like Shrubs with Bluish-black Fruit

Wild olive, fruit.

Cultivated olive, flowers.

WILD OLIVE

Olea europaea var. *sylvestris* · Oleaceae

Wild olive, fruit.

The olive branch is a well-known symbol of peace. Found throughout the Mediterranean region, the wild variety is appealing for its rarity and exceptional longevity. The far more common cultivated variety *Olea europaea* var. *europaea* is a fixture of the Mediterranean landscape, where olive groves and stalls selling bottles of olive oil can be found around every corner. A large number of cultivars have been developed for cultivation.

The plant's gnarled trunk is topped by a characteristic, open crown. Its branches bear evergreen leaves and are covered in slightly prickly bark. The oblong, opposite, lance-shaped leaves are lighter underneath. Its whitish **flowers** stand somewhat erect and form racemes at the leaf joints. The calyx is made up of four small lobes and the corolla has four wide-spreading oval petals. The **fruit** takes the form of an elongated fleshy drupe which turns from green to black when ripe. The flesh is rich in fat and surrounds a single hard stone.

↕	2–3 m
✸	February/June
🍒	August/September
▲▲	0–700 m
👄	Edible

Phillyrea media, flowers.

Mock privet, fruit.

Mock privet, flowers.

Phillyrea latifolia · Oleaceae

Depending on its specific habitat and age, the plant can grow to different sizes and its leaves can take on different shapes. For a long time, this variability was explained using distinct sub-species and debate rages on today in discussion boards on botanical websites. Whatever the details of its classification, the plant's tight-grained wood makes excellent charcoal.

The plant's trunk, which has plenty of bends and curves, supports sturdy, opposite branches that form a thick crown. Its oval, opposite, lance-shaped leaves are 2 cm wide and have small spiny teeth along their edges. Its first leaves and those at bottom of the stems are heart-shaped at the base. Up to 12 pairs of lateral veins are visible on the leaves. The narrower, upper leaves have a prominent dorsal vein. The small number of tiny yellowish **flowers** form little clusters at the leaf joints. Its **fruit** takes the form of small black drupes which are slightly flattened at their ends and contain a round stone.

Mock privet, fruit.

↕	4–8 m
☀	April/May
◖◗	August/September
▲▲	0–700 m
🗙	Unpalatable

Tree-like Shrubs with Bluish-black Fruit

Damson, flowers.

DAMSON

Prunus domestica subsp. *insititia* · Rosaceae

Damson, fruit.

The many varieties of this plant are widespread throughout the hedgerows of Europe. Damsons can be used in the same way as their close relation the sloe to make a flavoured gin. Unlike sloes, however, they can be eaten raw or made into puddings in the same way as plums.

The damson's new and second-year stems are hairy. A small number of thorns are scattered on the plant. Its deciduous, oval leaves have dentate edges and are covered in small downy hairs underneath. They appear at the same time as the white **flowers**, which are found singly or in pairs, and have hairy peduncles. The **fruit** takes the form of roundish, purplish-blue or sometimes reddish drupes, which are covered in a whitish bloom. The flesh remains stubbornly attached to its smooth stone. The species is often used as stock for grafting.

↕	5–6 m
✳	April/May
🍒	July/October
⛰	0–1000 m
👄	Edible

Damson, branch and new leaves.

Damson, branches in bloom.

Cherry laurel, flowers.

CHERRY LAUREL

Prunus laurocerasus · Rosaceae

Cherry laurel, fruit.

This laurel grows in open beech and oak woods in milder climates or as a hedging plant elsewhere. Since its introduction to Europe in the 16th century, the species has adapted well – perhaps too well, as the shadows cast by the shrubs can compromise the growth of other plant species and its invasive nature is being monitored in some regions. There is certainly no shortage of the plant, which is used to produce laurel water.

The cherry laurel's hairless, undulating stems are initially greenish until they eventually take on a grey colour. Its long, oval, lance-shaped, alternate leaves are relatively thick. They are a glossy dark green, lighter on the underside, with entire edges, and give off a characteristic bitter almond odour when bruised. The many white **flowers** form long racemes and there is sometimes a second flowering in autumn. The **fruit** takes the form of shiny, oval drupes that change colour from red to black and measure 8–15 mm in diameter. Even a few are sufficient to cause a serious case of poisoning, so take care not to confuse the plant with other laurels, and particularly, do not mistake its leaves for bay leaves.

↕	5–6 m
✳	April/June
🍒	August/October
⛰	0–600 m
☠	Toxic

Prunus padus subsp. petraea, fruit.

Bird cherry, flowers.

Prunus padus · Rosaceae

Bird cherry, fruit.

Also known as hackberry, this plant produces fruit with a rather astringent taste and the wood gives off an unpleasant odour when chopped. Its abundance of flowers make for an attractive display and are readily pollinated by insects, while birds provide effective dispersal for the stones found within its fruit. A rare plant, it can be found in damp and partly shaded areas.

The plant's stems readily produce suckers. Its deciduous, oval, lance-shaped, alternate leaves are 6–8 cm in length, with finely dentate edges and, on the underside, clearly visible veins. Long racemes of strongly scented **flowers** grow out horizontally, appearing with the leaves, and curve as they mature. The small corolla is composed of white petals. Bird cherry produces **fruit** in the form of small, shiny black drupes which measure 6–9 mm in diameter and are produced in clusters. Each drupe contains a ridged stone.

DID YOU KNOW?

Prunus padus subsp. *petraea* or
Prunus padus subsp. *borealis*
Prominent veins are visible on the undersides of the leaves. Its yellowish flowers form upright racemes and its fruit are found in upright or wide-spreading clusters.

∿

↕	4–12 m
☀	April/May
🜘	July/August
⛰	100–1800 m
🐛	Unpalatable

Tree-like Shrubs with Bluish-black Fruit

Alpine buckthorn, flowers.

ALPINE BUCKTHORN

Rhamnus alpina · Rhamnaceae

Alpine buckthorn, fruit.

After an avalanche, falling rocks, or other dramatic changes to the landscape in alpine regions of Europe, the alpine buckthorn is among the first species to colonize these cleared spaces. It has a distinct preference for warm, sunny spots with chalky soil. It is found among snowy mespilus and junipers on rocky heaths and in rock fissures that contain organic matter. The plant is not damaged by heavy snowfall as its supple branches bend under the weight and stand upright slowly again in spring.

The plant has a twisting trunk and thornless branches with reddish-brown bark. It is a dioecious plant, with male and female reproductive organs on separate plants. Its deciduous, oval, dentate leaves are fairly long (5–8 cm) and many slightly curved veins are clearly visible on its darker underside. Very small unisexual greenish **flowers** form bunches just above where the leaves meet the branches. The flowers are composed of four petals and four sepals. The **fruit** takes the form of green drupes (5–7 mm) which progressively ripen to crimson and then glossy black.

↕	1.5–3 m
☀	May/June
🍒	August/September
▲▲	500–1600 m
☠	Toxic

Purging buckthorn, female flowers.

Purging buckthorn, male flowers.

Rhamnus catharticus · Rhamnaceae

There is a long history of tinctures of purging buckthorn, or common buckthorn, mixed with other ingredients to make an herbal laxative. Green colouring can also be extracted from the fruit and mixed with lime or alum to produce a dye. The plant's yellowish, striped, hard, compact wood was employed in furniture manufacturing, sculpture, and inland woodwork, and is still used today to lend a fiery hue to works of art. The plant is also commonly known as rainberry thorn, common hart's horn, and waythorn.

The branches are thorny, particularly at the ends. The large, often opposite leaves are slightly dentate, with four pairs of curved veins. The petioles are roughly half the length of the leaves. The male or female **flowers** form small bunches, their calyces composed of four pointed lobes, while the greenish corollas consist of four 5–6 mm long petals. The **fruit** takes the form of round, shiny drupes, which turn from green to black and form regular clusters at the base of young shoots. They are 5–8 mm in diameter and contain four stones.

Purging buckthorn, fruit.

↕	3–5 m
☀	May/June
♠	September/October
▲▲	0–1600 m
✖	Slightly toxic

Dwarf buckthorn, flowers.

DWARF BUCKTHORN

Rhamnus pumila · Rhamnaceae

Dwarf buckthorn, fruit.

The smallest member of the *Rhamnus* family, this plant is the best adapted to high altitudes and difficult growing conditions. It can be found growing in the company of glacier buttercup, among rocks, on scree-covered slopes, and in cracks at altitudes of 3000 m. Neither cold, nor frost, nor snow prevents it from flowering and bearing fruit. One of the benefits of living at such a high altitude is that it is rarely disturbed.

The plant's silvery-grey twisted trunk creeps along the surfaces of rocks and bears knotty branches with several offshoots. Its small, slightly curved leaves are dark green on top and have 4–7 pairs of very prominent secondary veins. The edges of the leaves are finely dentate and attached to the branches via short petioles. The very small, male or female, greenish-white **flowers** are easy to miss. They are distributed evenly throughout the plant in clusters of three or four. The corolla is composed of four petals and the calyx of four pointed lobes. The plant's **fruit** takes the form of berries, 5–8 mm in diameter, which change from dark red to black and contrast with the adjacent foliage and rock surfaces. The fruit is slightly toxic and contains three seeds.

↕	10–20 cm
✳	June/July
⚭	September/October
▲▲	1100–3100 m
⚹	Toxic

Wayfaring tree, flowers.

Viburnum lantana · Caprifoliaceae

The dense, flexible wood of the wayfaring tree is used in wickerwork, while in its natural setting, the tree brightens up hedges on dreary autumn days with its multi-coloured clusters of fruit. Not to be outdone by the fruit, the plant's pretty spring flowers form massive white bunches. These features have not escaped the attention of horticulturists, who have created a number of interesting cultivars from the wild plant, producing viburnums that have colourful leaves in autumn, that flower in winter, or that have orange fruit.

The plant's brown bark becomes grey and cracked with age and the hairy, opposite branches have a large number of curves. Its thick, long (10–12 cm), oval leaves are dentate, with prominent veins, and are greyish-green underneath. The **flowers** have a pleasant aroma and form large corymbs (8–10 cm); they have a white corolla with rounded petals, long stamens, and a hairy pedicel. Its **fruit** takes the form of oval drupes (7–9 mm) with two slightly flattened sides, initially red and ripening to a purplish-black colour. They ripen at varying rates and thus its fruit clusters often contain different-coloured drupes at various stages of maturity. The plant is also commonly known as cotton tree, lithy tree, and twistwood.

Wayfaring tree, fruit.

↕	2–3 m
☀	May/June
⚭	August/Mid-October
⚠	0–1400 m
☣	Slightly toxic

Fig, flowers (cross-section of the receptacle).

FIG

Ficus carica · Moraceae

Fig, fruit.

Figs were introduced to Britain, France, and other parts of Europe by the Romans. These vestiges of the ancient empire produce sweet fruit that is rich in vitamins. Ripe figs make excellent jams, on their own or mixed with other fruit, and are eaten raw to accompany many dishes. They can be baked into pies, tarts, and cakes, roasted with meat, or used to make liqueurs and cocktails.

The plant's ash-grey bark has a more or less uniform appearance. Its fragile branches are easily broken and contain a milky pith. The edges of its thick, alternate leaves are deeply cut into 3–7 undulate lobes. The leaves are rough to the touch and measure 15 cm in length. Its hermaphroditic (with both male and female reproductive organs) **flowers** are hidden inside a pear-shaped receptacle turned inside out (see the photograph above). The plants are pollinated thanks to a small insect known as the fig wasp, in what is a rather complicated process. The green to purplish-brown fruit-bearing structure is a false fruit, which measures 6–7 cm in length. The true **fruit** are small aggregate drupes which are found inside and contain the seeds.

↕	2–7 m
✳	June/September
⚭	August/September
▲▲	0–800 m
👄	Edible

Spanish juniper, flowers.

SPANISH JUNIPER

Juniperus thurifera · Cupressaceae

Incense was the traditional offering used to honour St Crispin. When the aromatic resin was in short supply, it was replaced with wood from the Spanish juniper. The plant was also used to decontaminate homes following epidemics. Some ancient specimens have twisted, bent trunks that give a palpable sense of the plant's age, and the few sites where this remarkably long-lived species grows must be preserved.

Spanish juniper, fruit.

The plant's somewhat dense young twisting shoots develop into well-defined branches. Its leaves, which are initially short and lance-shaped, turn into triangular scales. They are arranged in many rows and give the stems a slightly square appearance. The plant's discreet male and female **flowers** are found on separate plants and are well protected by scales. Its **fruit** takes the form of a round false berry (galbulus), which is 8–12 mm in diameter and turns from greenish-grey to blue and finally to a blackish colour when ripe. The surface appears dented and it contains 3–4 bumpy seeds. Like the savin, another member of the juniper family, the entire plant is toxic.

↕	3–6 m
☀	March/May
🍒	September/October
⛰	400–1200 m
☠	Toxic

Tree-like Shrubs with Bluish-black Fruit

Common juniper, female flowers.

Common juniper, male flowers.

COMMON JUNIPER

Juniperus communis · Cupressaceae

Common juniper, fruit.

Nowadays, juniper berries are rarely used in recipes, in spite of their well-recognized digestive and fortifying properties. Nonetheless, food lovers do still occasionally enjoy them in marinades and traditional sauerkraut. The berries make an excellent accompaniment to pheasant or venison and are also used flavour gin.

The plant's many branches, which retain their green colour, form bushes that grow somewhat upright. Its small, needle-shaped leaves are clustered in groups of three. The plant's barely visible **flowers** are grouped in small cones which are protected by scales; the male flower cones contain the pollen sacs and the females house one or several ovaries. It is a dioecious species, with male and female reproductive organs on separate plants. The plant's **fruit** resemble small berries, but in fact are dry fruit known as galbuluses, which can vary from 5 to 10 mm in size. The fruit are greenish the first year and ripen to blackish-blue the following year. It is common to see fruit at various stages of ripeness on the same plant.

↕	2–4 m
☀	April/May
⚭	September/March
⛰	0–1800 m
👄	Edible

DID YOU KNOW?

J. communis subsp. *nana* or *Juniperus sibirica*
This low-spreading evergreen shrub has thick, twisting branches with straight tips. Its needle-shaped leaves are less prickly and it is exceptionally long-lived.

∾

RECIPE

═══════ JUNIPER TEA ═══════

Harvesting
Pick only the fully ripe, dark blue fruit after the first frosts. Dehydrate them in a dry spot and store them in a tin once dried.

Therapeutic properties
The berries are traditionally used for their diuretic and antibacterial effects on the urinary tract. They also aid digestion.

Method and directions for use
In a small saucepan, pour water over the berries (roughly 5 g per cup) and allow to simmer for 4–5 minutes. Allow to cool and sieve the liquid. Serve with honey at the end of a meal.

RECIPE

═══════ JUNIPER BERRY SAUCE ═══════

Ingredients
20 g juniper berries
10 g butter
1 small shallot, finely chopped
Parsley

Method
Crush the berries with a pestle and mortar.
Melt the butter in a pan and add the finely chopped shallot and the parsley.
Add the juniper berries.
Continue to cook for 1 minute. The sauce can be served as an accompaniment to veal kidneys, wild game, or roasted pigeon.

J. communis subsp. *nana* or *Juniperus sibirica*, fruit.

J. communis subsp. *nana* or *Juniperus sibirica*, shrub (low-spreading).

Tree-like Shrubs with Bluish-black Fruit

Service tree, fruit.

TREES

Trees are defined by their hard trunks and branches, which get their rigidity from lignin, the main component of wood. Adult trees grow to be greater than 7 m in height, and the lower parts of their trunks are generally free of branches, with a few exceptions (for example common yew and rowan). The terminal branches that bear the leaves are collectively known as the crown.

Persimmon, flowers.

PERSIMMON

Diospyros kaki · Ebenaceae

Persimmon, fruit.

Native to Asia, this plant was introduced to Europe at the end of the 18th century. Late in autumn, it puts on a spectacular display of colour, after which the tree sheds its leaves, leaving behind a multitude of round yellow, orange, or coppery-brown fruit on its branches. The fruit remain in place until thrushes and other birds set their sights on the delicious source of nourishment. It grows in Britain only as a garden plant and needs a long, hot summer to set fruit.

The persimmon is a species with distinct male and female plants. Its greyish bark flakes off easily. The large (6–15 cm), leathery, oval leaves end in a sharp point, the glossy upper parts contrasting with the hairier undersides. The plant's inconspicuous pale yellow **flowers**, which are arranged in cymes, are made up of a calyx composed of hairy sepals and a corolla with curved petals. Its **fruit** takes the form of large berries (8–10 cm) which turn from green to orange to a reddish colour. Rich in vitamin C, they can only be consumed when overripe, at which point the flesh is juicy and sweet. Many flat, oval, brownish seeds are found inside the berries.

↕	7–10 m
✸	Mid–May/June
⚬⚬	October/November
▲▲	0–500 m
◡	Edible

Wild cherry, flowers (detail).

Wild cherry, tree in bloom.

WILD CHERRY

Prunus avium · Rosaceae

A favourite of birds, the cherries that can be picked before they strip the tree can be eaten raw (in moderation) or steeped in strong liquor, such as brandy (with added sugar), to extract the subtle flavour. The first attempts at developing cherry brandy can be traced to the 16th century; by the beginning of the 20th century, trade in it was booming. Kirsch is produced through a double distillation of fermented fruit, resulting in a delicate white liqueur.

The plant's straight trunk is topped by an average-sized crown. With time, its light brown bark peels off in wide strips. Its large, alternate, oval leaves, irregularly dentate and somewhat hairy underneath, have long (3–5 cm) petioles with reddish veins. The **flowers**, which have white oval petals, hang on long pedicels, forming tight bunches that bloom just before the leaves start to unfold. Its **fruit**, the wild cherry, is a dark red drupe with bitter-tasting flesh that surrounds a smooth stone.

Wild cherry, fruit.

↕	15–25 m
☀	April/May
🍒	July/August
▲▲	0–1500 m
👄	Edible

Trees

Jujube, flowers.

JUJUBE

Ziziphus zizyphus · Rhamnaceae

Jujube, fruit.

Some insect species feed only on very specific types of plants. Such is the case of the Mediterranean fruit fly (*Ceratitis capitata*), which is very fond of jujubes. To protect the plants, pheromone traps, which contain compounds that are identical to natural hormones to deceive the insects, can be used. Alternatively, they can be kept at bay through the use of appropriate insecticides.

Also known as red date or Chinese date, this small tree has brownish bark that gradually cracks. Its branches vary in appearance, some of them thick, twisting, thorny, and growing in zigzags, while others are more slender and slightly curved. Its deciduous, entire, alternate, oval leaves are arranged in two opposite rows. The leaves are glossy, with three converging main veins running through them. The plant produces tiny yellowish **flowers** at the leaf joints. The star-shaped corolla has five pointed lobes, inside which are five stamens surrounding a single style that emerges from a central disc. Its **fruit**, jujubes, are small, fleshy, olive-shaped drupes, which are 5 cm long and initially greenish yellow, ripening to reddish-brown. A thin skin covers the sweet-tasting flesh, which contains a single stone. The fruit make a tasty snack.

↕	6–8 m
✴	April/May
◐◖	September
▲▲	0–600 m
👄	Edible

Hackberry, green fruit.

Nettle tree, flowers.

NETTLE TREE

Celtis australis · Ulmaceae

In France this tree's wood has a long history of being made into three-pronged pitchforks, a practice that stretches back to the 12th century. There is even a museum devoted to the craft in the village of Sauve, in France. Wood turners and sculptors also appreciate the wood's unique qualities.

Hardy and frost-resistant, the tree's trunk is covered in thin, dark grey bark. Its many light, flexible branches form a crown with a rounded shape. Its oval, lance-shaped, asymmetrical, alternate leaves are rather rough on top and downy underneath. The upper half is roughly dentate. The plant's small number of solitary, greenish-yellow **flowers** are supported by long pedicels. Its **fruit** takes the form of a round drupe, roughly the size of a small cherry, which changes from green to a rusty brown to black. The fruit has a particularly bitter taste, which makes it inedible.

Nettle tree, fruit.

DID YOU KNOW?

Hackberry – *Celtis occidentalis*
The tree features scaly bark and the leaf margins are dentate nearly all the way around.

↕	10–20 m
✳	April/Mid-May
🫐	August/September
▲▲	0–1000 m
🦋	Unpalatable

Oleaster, flowers.

OLEASTER

Elaeagnus angustifolia · Elaeagnaceae

Oleaster, fruit.

On windy days, the oleaster's leaves turn over to reveal their radiant silvery undersides. This brilliance is due to the presence of small light grey scales on the surface. The tree's crown vibrates in the wind and the reflection of the sun's light gives it a striking frosted appearance, particularly on mid-summer days.

Naturalized in sandy coastal areas, the oleaster has been planted elsewhere to prevent soil erosion and to act as a windbreak. Its younger branches are grey and scaly, while the older ones are brownish. Some have thorns, while others have none. The tree's oblong, lance-shaped leaves are green on top and metallic grey underneath. Its particularly fragrant yellow **flowers** feature a perianth made up of four triangular tepals that form a bell shape. Its **fruit** takes the form of brownish drupes punctuated with silvery marks. They contain a single stone, measure 1–1.5 cm in diameter and have a sweet taste. They can also be dried.

↕	4–10 m
☀	June/July
⚬⚬	September/October
▲▲	0–800 m
⬯	Edible

DID YOU KNOW?

Elaeagnus × ebbingei is a popular landscaping plant that produces speckled jelly bean-like fruit from April to May. It is planted in the most unlikely of places, such as the central reservation leading to Heathrow airport and Plymouth city centre.

Wild Fruit

Common walnut, male flowers.

Common walnut, female flowers.

COMMON WALNUT

Juglans regia · Juglandaceae

Common walnut, fruit.

ultivated since Roman times, this Eurasian species replaced a more ancient, less productive variety, which has been found on archaeological sites. The tree grows readily in certain alluvial woods and other locations. It is primarily used as a food source, though its wood is highly coveted by cabinetmakers. The plant has very fragile leaves, which appear only late in the spring and drop at the first signs of wintry weather in autumn. The tree has an imposing height and is exceptionally long-lived, with a life span of two to four centuries.

The trunk, which is covered in light grey bark, supports a thin, rounded crown made up of large branches. Its alternate leaves are divided into 5–9 leaflets, whose terminal leaflet is longer. The petioles are distinctly thicker at the base. Tiny female **flowers** appear on the year's new branches, while the male flowers form elongated racemes on the previous year's growth. The **fruit** takes the form of a drupe made up of a fleshy pale green husk that envelops the nut.

Black walnut, fruit.

DID YOU KNOW?

Black walnut – *Juglans nigra*
The plant's leaves are made up of 8–11 pairs of leaflets. Its sections of fruit are fused together.

↕	15–25 m
☀	April/May
🌢	September/ October
⛰	0–1000 m
👄	Edible

White cedar, autumn fruit.

White cedar, flowers.

WHITE CEDAR

Melia azedarach · Meliaceae

White cedar, fruit.

Also known as Indian lilac, this plant was introduced to mainland Europe in the 17th century. It requires long periods of sun to develop properly. The plant's leaves and bark have purgative properties, while the dried stones of its round, marble-like fruit were used in making rosaries, which is why it is also known as bead tree.

The tree's brownish and purplish bark forms vertical cracks. Its deciduous, alternate leaves are divided into long dentate leaflets. The plant's purple lilac-coloured flowers, which hang on thin pedicels, form long panicles. The **flowers** have a star-shaped corolla made up of five oblong petals that surround a column of stamens and release a distinct odour when rubbed. The **fruit** consists of yellowish-brown, oval drupes, which are 12–15 mm in diameter. They remain on the plant long after it has shed its foliage.

↕	10–15 m
✱	March/June
🍒	September/December
▲▲	0–500 m
☠	Toxic

Black cherry, flowers.

BLACK CHERRY

Prunus serotina · Rosaceae

The black cherry is native to North America, where it grows in more than two-thirds of its states, mainly in the west. It is not found in Britain, but has naturalized in many mainland European countries, including France, Germany, Denmark, and Poland. The ecological and economic consequences of the plant's introduction are currently being measured and the information will help with the management of the species.

The blackish-grey bark of the black cherry is punctuated with small brown outgrowths on the young branches. The leathery, oval, dentate leaves taper to a point; they have a central vein covered with brownish downy hairs and are glossy on top and more matt underneath. The tree produces 10–12 cm racemes of white **flowers** with rounded petals at the end of long peduncles. Each flower is supported by a short pedicel (4–6 cm). The **fruit** takes the form of small drupes, which turn from red to black, and contain a smooth stone surrounded by bitter-tasting flesh.

Black cherry, fruit.

↕	12–30 m
☀	June/July
🍒	September/October
⛰	0–800 m
🌿	Unpalatable

Trees

Mahaleb cherry, flowers.

MAHALEB CHERRY

Prunus mahaleb · Rosaceae

Mahaleb cherry, fruit.

When the wood of this tree is broken, it releases a pleasant aroma. It is highly coveted for use in woodwork, cabinetmaking, sculpture, and even the manufacture of canes and handles. Long ago, in a monastery dedicated to Saint Lucia in the region of Vosges, France, Franciscan monks gained renown for the stunning work they produced using the wood. This explains why the plant is sometimes referred to as St Lucie cherry.

The tree's thick trunk, from which its straight branches emerge, is covered in blackish-grey bark that tends to form cracks. Its small (5–6 cm), oval, alternate, dentate leaves are slightly creased along their main vein. There are nectar glands on the upper part of the petioles. The profuse, small, slightly fragrant, white **flowers** (8–12 mm) form short, loose racemes; the corolla has distinctly separate petals. The plant's **fruit** takes the form of small spherical drupes, roughly the size of a pea. These mini cherries contain a single stone and change colour from reddish to black. The fruit have a tart flavour.

↕	6–10 m
☀	April
⚬⚬	August
▲▲	0–1500 m
👄	Edible

White mulberry, fruit.

White mulberry, flowers.

BLACK MULBERRY

Morus nigra · Moraceae

The fruit of the black mulberry bears a striking resemblance to the blackberries produced by wild brambles – so much so that it is often mistakenly referred to as blackberries rather than mulberries. The similarities end there, as one is produced by a tree and the other by a shrub. Botanically speaking, the mulberry belongs to the genus *Morus*, while the blackberry is of the genus *Rubus*. However, they are united in the fact that the fruit of both species is cherished by food-lovers.

The tree's trunk produces many branches. Its thick, hairy, dentate leaves are heart-shaped and quite rough to the touch. Spikes of sessile **flowers** remain hidden beneath the foliage. It is a monoecious species, with both male and female reproductive organs on the same plant. Its **fruit** takes the form of oblong drupelets, which are initially red and ripen to black. They have a pleasant, refreshing taste.

Black mulberry, fruit.

Black mulberry, flowers.

DID YOU KNOW?

White mulberry – *Morus alba*
The plant's leaves are the preferred food of silkworms and thus have long been vital to silk production. Its fruit are of a pinkish colour.

~⌒~

↕	5–15 m
✳	April/June
🝆	Mid-June/September
⛰	0–800 m
👄	Edible

Common whitebeam, flowers.

COMMON WHITEBEAM

Sorbus aria · Rosaceae

Common whitebeam, fruit.

On windy days this tree puts on an attractive display, as its leaves are lifted to reveal their silvery undersides. This natural feature of the leaves can be seen from far away, and is perhaps why the tree is often favoured by landscape architects. The plant is used to spruce up city streets and copes well with the pollution produced by passing vehicles.

The tree's straight trunk is covered in grey, nearly smooth bark, and is topped by a rounded crown. Its leathery, alternate, oval leaves (8–12 cm) are unevenly dentate, with a glossy green upper surface contrasting with the whitish, hairy undersides. Its white **flowers** (12–15 mm) form compact, flattened corymbs. The petals and downy styles surround stamens with yellow anthers. Its **fruit**, known as a sorb, is a roundish (8–12 mm), orange-red false fruit with a grainy surface and a floury taste.

↕	3–15 m
✹	May/June
♠	September/October
▲▲	0–1800 m
👄	Edible

DID YOU KNOW?

Sorbus aria var. *nivea*
The plant's leaves are downy on both sides.

∿∿

RECISE

SORB CAKE

Harvesting
Pick the overripe fruit of the common whitebeam and wild service tree,
between the end of September and mid-October.

Ingredients
1 kg red and brown sorbs
400 g sugar
200 g butter
2 eggs
250 g flour
pinch of ginger
pinch of salt
1 tablespoon yeast

Method
Place the sorbs in a saucepan and cover with water.
Cook until the fruit can easily be squashed with a spatula.
Pass the fruit through a food mill and put aside.
Mix the sugar and butter. Add the eggs and the sorb purée.
Mix in the flour, ginger, salt, and yeast.
Pour the mixture into a buttered cake tin.
Bake at a moderate temperature for 30–40 minutes.
Allow to cool before serving.

Sorbus aria var. *nivea*, leaves.

Rowan, flowers.

ROWAN

Sorbus aucuparia · Rosaceae

Rowan, fruit.

The fruit of the rowan tree contains a sweet low-calorie compound known as sorbitol and attracts all manner of birds, particularly thrushes. People who need to keep their sugar consumption in check may also be tempted by the fleshy fruit, but its bitter taste, even after cooking, will probably dissuade them. Nonetheless, the fruit can be enjoyed in another form – a brandy which tastes vaguely of kirsch.

The plant's sometimes very short trunk varies in height and is topped by a rather dense, spreading crown. Fissures form readily on its greyish bark. Its alternate leaves are made up of 9–15 oblong, pointed leaflets which have fully dentate margins. Its many **flowers**, which form thick terminal bunches, have small white petals and three or four styles. The flowers give off a distinctive odour. Its small (7–10 mm) accessory **fruit** takes the form of red to orange-red sorbs that last long into winter.

↕	10–15 m
☀	May/June
♠	August/October
⛰	0–2000 m
👄	Edible

SORB WINE

Ingredients
1 kg common whitebeam sorbs
1 kg rowan sorbs
30 g baker's yeast
2 litres water
2 litres syrup (see below)

Method
Wash the sorbs and place them in a jar. Mix the yeast in a little lukewarm water and leave it to activate. Pour it into the jar with the remaining water. Allow the mixture to stand for a week, stirring each day. Strain the mixture into a demijohn and add 2 litres of slightly warmed syrup (prepare the syrup with equal weights of sugar and water: mix, heat to boiling point, boil for 30 seconds, and then allow to cool). The mixture will ferment, so keep a close eye on it. When the liquid floating on the surface becomes clear, decant the wine into bottles, seal thoroughly and store in a cool location. Consume quickly, in moderation.

Rowan, fruit clusters.

Service tree, flowers.

Service tree, apple-shaped fruit.

SERVICE TREE

Sorbus domestica · Rosaceae

Service tree, fruit.

The wood of this tree is harder than oak and is remarkably even and dense. These qualities were once valued for manufacturing parts for mechanical gears or large press screws, and the service tree was planted along roads both for ornament and as a source material. Nowadays, it is still used in cabinetmaking, inlaid work, and to make parts for pianos and other musical instruments.

It is a large tree that can reach 20 m in height, with a rounded crown. Its straight trunk is covered in blackish-grey bark with regular scaly patches. Its leaves have long petioles and are divided into 11–21 leaflets, the top two-thirds of which are dentate. The plant's **flowers**, which form tight bunches, are characterized by their white corolla, five styles, and stamens which are longer than the petals. Its small (2–3 cm) yellowish and purplish-red accessory **fruit**, in the shape of a small pear (var. *pyrifera*), are known as sorbs. They become edible when over-ripe, though they retain their astringent flavour.

↕	6–20 m
✳	April/June
🍂	September/October
⛰	0–1500 m
👄	Edible

DID YOU KNOW?

Sorbus domestica var. *pomifera*
Its small fruit are apple-shaped.

〜〜

Wild service tree, fruit.

WILD SERVICE TREE

Sorbus torminalis · Rosaceae

This tree's fruit can be transformed into brandy and its wood is used in a number of different applications thanks to its many desirable qualities, including its evenness, hardness, and colour. Sculptors, cabinetmakers, and wood wholesalers are very fond of the wood, as are manufacturers of musical instruments, billiard cues, and guns. Its astringent fruit can soothe stomach pains, from which the Latin origin of its botanical name *tominalis* derives.

The tree's grey bark is covered in small brownish outgrowths, known as lenticels. Its entire, alternate leaves have sharply triangular lobes which narrow towards the tip. Three to five lateral veins are visible on the leaves, which are darker on top and are attached to the branches by long, slender petioles. The plant's **flowers** (10–12 mm), which are arranged in cymes at the end of short stems, have white corollas with rounded petals. The two styles at the base of the flowers are surrounded by prominent stamens. The accessory **fruit** takes the form of oval berries (12–15 mm) that ripen from brownish-green to brown and are covered in small greyish bumps. They are edible after the first frosts, as long as their tart flavour is acceptable.

Wild service tree, flowers.

↕	10–15 m
☀	May/June
♠	September/October
⛰	0–1200 m
👄	Edible

Broad-leaved whitebeam, flowers.

Sorbus remensis Cornier, leaves.

BROAD-LEAVED WHITEBEAM

Sorbus × latifolia · Rosaceae

Broad-leaved whitebeam, fruit.

Also known as the service tree of Fontainebleau, the species originated in the Fountainebleu forest, southeast of Paris. It shows a distinct preference for warm, dry spots in open woods and along forest fringes. It is a naturally occurring hybrid that results from the crossing of *Sorbus aria* and *Sorbus torminalis* and as it is a stable hybrid, the plant can reproduce.

The tree's size can vary tremendously depending on its habitat. Its branches are covered in brownish bark and bear leaves that are large at the base and narrow progressively towards the tip. They are dentate, hairless on top and hairy underneath, have clearly visible veins and are attached to the branches by short petioles. White **flowers** are borne in small cymes at the ends of the branches. The corolla and calyx are open, revealing two styles. The tree's inedible accessory **fruit** are small (1–1.5 cm), oval, and reddish-brown in colour.

↕	3–12 m
✳	May
⚭	August
⛰	200–600 m
✖	Unpalatable

DID YOU KNOW?

Sorbus remensis **Cornier**
This new microspecies results from the crossing of service trees discovered by B. Cornier.

~✎~

Common yew, female flowers.

Common yew, male flower.

COMMON YEW

Taxus baccata · Taxaceae

The common yew's evergreen foliage and the shape of its leaves are reminiscent of a variety of pine tree. However, on closer inspection, it becomes clear that its fruit are not cones, but rather small, round, red balls that resemble berries. The species is rare in natural habitats, but is often planted in gardens, parks and churchyards, where it can be topiarized. Another unusual characteristic of the plant is its exceptional longevity – its slow growth can continue for more than a thousand years. The common yew can adapt to all types of soil, including chalky, shaded, sunny, dry, or damp. It is also known as English yew.

The tree's brownish bark gradually exfoliates. Its evergreen leaves are reduced to flattened needles of varying lengths (1.5–2.5 cm), which are lighter underneath and are borne in two opposite rows. It is a dioecious species, with male and female reproductive organs on separate plants. The greenish male **flowers** are more numerous and are arranged in small compact clusters, while its single or paired female flowers appear in small catkins. The tree's accessory **fruit** resembles a small berry. The fleshy red part is edible, but the seed found within it is very toxic, as are the plant's leaves and stems.

Common yew, fruit.

↕	5–15 m
☀	March/April
⚬⚬	September/November
▲▲	200–1500 m
☠	Toxic

Common honeysuckle, flowers.

APPENDICES

GLOSSARY OF BOTANICAL TERMS

- **Accessory fruit:** A fruit in which some of the flesh comes not from the ovary but from tissue at the exterior of the carpel.
- **Achene:** A dry fruit which contains a single seed.
- **Alternate:** Leaves or flowers borne at different levels of a stem.
- **Anther:** The tip of the stamen which contains the pollen.
- **Axillary:** Appearing at the upper angle of where the leaf stalk meets the stem or branch.
- **Berry:** A fleshy fruit that contains one or several seeds.
- **Blade:** The flat part of a leaf.
- **Bloom:** A thin layer of a greyish substance on the surface of a fruit.
- **Bract:** A small leafy or scaly growth.
- **Calycule:** A collection of outgrowths that resemble sepals, which appear outside the calyx.
- **Calyx:** The generally green outer part of the flower, which is made up of the sepals.
- **Capsule:** A dry fruit that breaks open.
- **Cladophyll:** A round or flattened leaf-like projection of a stem.
- **Cone:** An array of overlapping scales which contain the seeds of a conifer.
- **Corolla:** The petals that make up the inner part of the flower, which are often very colourful.
- **Corymb:** An inflorescence where all of the flowers sit in the same horizontal plane on pedicels of differing lengths.
- **Crampon:** An outgrowth allowing a plant to attach to its support.
- **Crown:** The collection of boughs and branches that are supported by the trunk of a tree or shrub.
- **Cupule:** A cup-shaped structure at the tip of certain fruits.
- **Cyme:** An inflorescence defined by a short main axis that branches out.

- **Deciduous:** Plant parts, typically leaves, that are shed.
- **Dentate:** With a toothed edge.
- **Dioecious:** A plant species in which male and female flowers are on different plants.
- **Downy:** Covered in small hairs.
- **Drupe:** A fleshy fruit that contains a stone with a single seed.
- **Drupelet:** A small drupe that forms part of an aggregation that makes up a compound fruit.
- **False fruit:** Another name for an accessory fruit.
- **Galbulus:** A hard, round fruit of conifers that resembles a berry.
- **Glandular:** Containing a gland or glands.
- **Inflorescence:** A collection of flowers found on a plant.
- **Lance-shaped:** Narrow and pointed at the end.
- **Leaflet:** A sub-section of the leaf blade of a compound leaf.
- **Lenticel:** A small outgrowth on bark.
- **Lobe:** A portion of a leaf that results from the incomplete division of the leaf's blade.
- **Monoecious:** A plant that has both male and female flowers on the same plant.
- **Needle:** A very slender, prickly leaf.
- **Panicle:** A compound raceme that forms a cone shape.
- **Pedicel:** A stalk that bears a flower and then a fruit.
- **Peduncle:** The stalk that bears an inflorescence and then a cluster of fruit.
- **Perennial:** A plant that lives for several years.
- **Perianth:** The outer part of a flower (calyx and corolla).
- **Petals:** The often very colourful flower parts that make up the corolla.
- **Petiole:** The slender part of a leaf that connects the blade to the branch or stem.

- **Pinnate:** Arranged on either side in pairs, opposite each other.
- **Pistil:** The female organs of a flower.
- **Prickle:** A pointed outgrowth on the bark of the plant, which is easily detached.
- **Raceme:** A collection of more or less tightly packed flowers attached to a central axis. The fruit they produce are also arranged in this way.
- **Reticulate:** A collection of veins that form a network.
- **Rhizome:** A thick underground stem.
- **Scale:** A thickened bract.
- **Sessile:** A leaf without a petiole or a flower without a pedicel.
- **Spadix:** A collection of small sessile flowers on an axis.
- **Spathe:** A membrane that partly covers an inflorescence.
- **Spike:** An inflorescence where the flowers sit side by side around a central axis.
- **Stamen:** The male organ of a flower.
- **Stipule:** A leafy outgrowth found at the base of the leaves, which sometimes occurs in pairs.

- **Stigma:** The tip of style, which receives the pollen.
- **Style:** An elongated part of the flower that connects the ovary to the stigma.
- **Stolon:** A creeping stem that can produce roots.
- **Sucker:** A shoot that emerges from a root.
- **Tendril:** A slender threadlike structure that allows a plant to attach itself to its support, either by coiling around it or with adhesive pads.
- **Tepal:** Flower parts where there is no differentiation between the sepals and the petals.
- **Terminal:** At the end of a stem or branch.
- **Thorn:** A pointed outgrowth of varying length that forms part of its support.
- **Tuberous:** Having a thickened root or underground stem.
- **Umbel:** An inflorescence where all of the flowers spring from the end of a stem.
- **Unisexual:** A flower that is either male or female.
- **Winged:** Having a thin lateral membranes.
- **Whorled:** Forming a circle around the same point on a stem.

Bayer, E., K.-P. Buttler, X. Finkenzeller, and J.Grau. *Guide de la flore méditerranéenne.* Neuchâtel and Paris: Delachaux et Niestlé, 1990.

Bertrand, A.-J., and B. Bertrand. *La Cuisine sauvage des haies et des talus.* Sengouagnet, France: Éditions de Terran, 2001.

Blamay, M., and C. Grey-Wilson. *La Flore d'Europe occidentale.* Paris: Éditions Arthaud, 1991; reprint Flammarion, 2003.

Brosse, J. *Larousse des arbres et des arbustes.* Paris: Éditions Larousse, 2000.

Calais, M. *Baies et petits fruits du bord des chemins.* Paris: Éditions du Chêne, 1998.

Chas, E., F. Le Driant, C. Dentant, L. Garraud, J. Vanes, P. Gillot, C. Remy, J.-C. Gattus, P. Salomez, and L. Quelin, illustrated by D. Mansion. *Atlas des plantes rares ou protégées des Hautes-Alpes.* Turriers, France: Naturalia Publications, 2006.

Da Costa, A., and F. Da Costa. *Jardins alpins, un parfum de paradis.* Grenoble: Libris, 2006.

Danesch, E., and O. Danesch. *Le Monde fascinant de la flore alpine.* Paris: Éditions Didier Richard, 1994.

De Belder, J., and X. Misonne. *Le Livre des baies.* Brussels: Éditions Racine, 1997.

Delahaye, T. *Les fruits rouges.* Paris: Actes Sud, 2002

Delahaye, T. *Les petits fruitiers des jardins.* Paris: Actes Sud, 2008.

Dreyer, E.-M. *Quelles sont ces baies et plantes sauvages?* Paris: Vigot, 2011.

Génevé, A., and M.-J.Génevé. *À la découverte des baies et fruits sauvages de Lorraine.* Metz, France: Éditions Serpenoise, 2002.

Girre, L. *Guide des baies toxiques des jardins et campagnes.* Neuchâtel and Paris: Delachaux et Niestlé, 2001.

Guillot, G., and J.-E. Roche. *Guides des fruits sauvages, fruits charnus.* Paris: Belin, 2010.

Jacob, I., and R. Sabatier. *Les Baies et autres petits fruits charnus.* Grenoble: Glénat, 1999.

Kremer, B. P. *Arbustes.* Paris: Fernand Nathan, 1996.

Laux, E.-L., and M. Guedes. *Baies et fruits de nos bois et jardins.* Paris: Bordas, 1982.

Lauber, K., and G. Wagner. *Flora Helvetica, flore illustrée de Suisse.* Paris: Belin, 2000.

Magnan, D., and H. Chaumeton. *Les plantes comestibles.* Paris: Éditions du Rocher, 1989.

More, D., and J. White. *Encyclopédie des arbres.* Paris: Flammarion, 2005.

Nardin, G. *Les Plantes sauvages.* Ingersheim: Editions S.A.E.P., 1988.

Parc national des Écrins, *Arbres et arbustes de montagne.* Grenoble: Libris, 2006.

Parc national des Écrins, *À la découverte des fleurs des Alpes.* Grenoble: Libris, 2002.

Polese, J.-M. *Encyclopédie visuelle des plantes sauvages.* Chamalières: Éditions Artémis, 2007.

Prades, J.-B., N. Prades, and G. Liege. *Le Grand Livre des fruits retrouvés.* Paris: Rustica Éditions, 2002.

Quinche, R. *Petit guide panoramique des fruits sauvages.* Neuchâtel and Paris: Delachaux et Niestlé, 1974.

Rameau, J.-C., D. Mansion and G. Dume. *Flore forestière française (Plaines et collines).* Paris: Institut pour le développement forestier, 1989.

Rameau, J.-C., D. Mansion and G. Dume. *Flore forestière française (Montagnes).* Paris: Institut pour le développement forestier, 1993.

Rameau, J.-C., D. Mansion, G. Dume and C. Gauberville. *Flore forestière française (Région méditerranéenne).* Paris: Institut pour le développement forestier, 2008.

Reynaud, J. *La flore du pharmacien.* Cachan, France: Éditions médicales internationales, 2002.

Schauenberg, P., and F. Paris. *Guide des plantes médicinales.* Neuchâtel and Paris: Delachaux et Niestlé, 1977.

Varlet, E. *Découvrez les fruits sauvages.* Paris: Éditions Sang de la Terre, 2008.

Vernier, F. and N. Lepeudry. *Glaner les fruits sauvages.* Courchevel Saint Bon, France: Tétras Éditions, 2009.

RECIPE INDEX

PHOTOGRAPHY CREDITS

All of the photographs in this book were taken by Alain Génevé, except the following:
- p.44 (bottom), p.67 (top left), p.127 (top), p 131 (top right), p.171 (bottom), p.207 (top left): Christian Bernard.
- p.21 (top right), p.204 (top left), p.204 (top right): Romuald Duda.
- p.49 (top left), p.177 (top): Jacques Fleurentin.
- p.112 (top left): Delphine Le Gac.
- p. 45 (top), p.117 (top right), p.183 (top right): Jean-Paul Maurice.
- p.201 (bottom): Albert Ortscheit.
- p.37 (top left), p.37 (top centre), p.38 (bottom), p.46 (top left), p.69 (top left), p.71 (bottom), p.79 (top left), p.83 (bottom), p.85 (top right), p.100 (bottom), p.104 (bottom), p.114 (bottom), p.117 (top left), p.123 (top), p.127 (bottom), p.137 (bottom), p.137 (top right), p.167 (top left), p.167 (top right), p.170 (top), p.182 (bottom), p.190 (bottom): Nicolas Pax.
- p.67 (top right), p.131 (top left): Aline Roth.
- p.122 (top right): Jean-Marie Weiss.

We sincerely thank all of these botanists and friends for their invaluable help and more particularly Christian Bernard and Nicolas Pax, who, through their knowledge and advice, have contributed to making this a better book.